THIN

BLOODY SO   wORKER

Richard Wills was born in 1967, in Whitehaven, Cumbria. He graduated in 1989 from Edge Hill University with a degree in Applied Social Sciences and went on to gain a Masters in Cultural Studies at Huddersfield University in 1996. He toiled in the social care sector for 32 years, qualifying as a social worker in 2004, before leaving the profession in 2020 feeling like a principled dinosaur. He is the youngest of three siblings, son of a teacher / steel worker and housewife / shop assistant. *Bloody Social Worker* is his first book, although he is currently writing a crime novel set in Oldham whilst studying to become a tutor in adult education.

'Bob Mullaly recently identified what he saw as a major shift in the 2005 social work Code of Ethics, in that reference to the social ideals of emancipation and humanitarianism had been removed. He interpreted this change as a retreat from the earlier version, which offered a more progressive vision of social justice and equality. The deletion leaves the profession to frame its societal role in the common-sense language of compassion. At issue here is not whether compassionate action is an important aspect of contemporary social work practices of care. Rather, without the modifying role of the social ideals, social workers are left susceptible in what Stjepan Mestrovic calls a "post-emotional society". Three concepts – individualization, virtue ethics, and active citizenship – may have direct influence on how today's social worker perceives, understands, and acts on social problems. The revised Code of Ethics, if left unchallenged, may help further subordinate the profession under the regressive structures of neo-liberalism.'

Colin R. Bonnycastle, *From Social Equality to Compassion*

'The criticism and humiliation heaped on social workers is limitless.'

Harry Ferguson, *The Guardian*

'In Rotherham (1997 – 2013) political correctness about race paralysed Police and social workers.'

Colin Brewer, *The Spectator*

'The reductive rhetoric of social workers "wading in", "doing too much", and being unduly interventionist serves a particular blow to the profession, just as "not doing enough" – particularly after a tragic outcome – can be equally as damaging to social work and to the families we work with.'

Andy Gill, *BASW* England Chair & Maris Stratulis, *BASW* England National Director

'Social workers get little glory – and they are burning out.'

Jason Lerner and Harold Pollack, *The Washington Post*

'Richard Wills provides a fascinating, down-to-earth account of the life and times of a mental health social worker. This book is a powerful antidote to the profession's more usual disparaged portrayal.'

Steve Rogowski, author of *Social Work: The Rise and Fall of a Profession?*

'Sometimes the greatest lessons and learnings are found in the simple retelling and examination of the everyday, of the ordinary, of the remains of our deeply introspective memories. An incredibly worthwhile read about 'us'.'

Juno Roche, author of *A Working Class Family Ages Badly*

'After an 18-year career in social work in Australia, New Zealand and England, I have now moved away from a client-facing role to back office policy and practice, having developed a sinking sense of hopelessness. This has come from fighting within a broken system which oppresses clients more than it supports positive change. Australia has a deep history of trauma, post-colonisation, and this has resulted in confusion around how services should respond to children in need without multiplying that trauma. I have seen misery and pain, and have been willing to give my all to fight for such a cause, but I now walk away with my own misery and pain given my inability to make a difference to those that need it. Richard Wills has walked away too, but not before trying his damnedest. *Bloody Social Worker* is a timely, powerful and poetic collection of stories which puts the lives of ordinary, often comical people, front and centre.'

Sarah Sulley née Waldram, Department of Communities, WA

'Wills takes us into an underground world, asks if we're still comfortable, and then splashes more heartache and humour onto the canvas irrespective of our answer. But these are places we simply have to go in order to understand what society has become.'

Ade Kolade, ex-researcher at the University of Manchester

'*Bloody Social Worker* removes the feeble, white vests of politicians, straps them into a ghost train and shows them the horrors of life at the bottom. It is not without the odd wink though, which kept Wills sane.'

Andrew Routledge

Richard Wills

BLOODY

SOCIAL

WORKER

THINKWELL BOOKS

Edited by Jeff Weston.
Cover design by Alejandro Baigorri.
Author guidance from Julianne Ingles.
Interior formatting by Rachel Bostwick.
Published by Thinkwell Books, U.K.
First printing edition 2022.

To the many dedicated souls working in Social Care.

You do the most important job in the world.

Never forget that.

"The scene is memory and is therefore non-realistic.
Memory takes a lot of poetic license.
It omits some details, others are exaggerated,
according to the emotional value of the article it touches,
for memory is seated predominantly in the heart."
- Tennessee Williams, *The Glass Menagerie*, 1944

CONTENTS

FOREWORD...xv

PREFACE..1

Chapter 1 - Teenage Discord.......................................9

Chapter 2 - Cedarmount Elderly Persons Home 21

Chapter 3 - Denton Road...37

Chapter 4 - Trade Union Work...................................51

Chapter 5 - Mr M...65

Chapter 6 - The Voluntary Sector 75

Chapter 7 - Mrs B 87

Chapter 8 - Secure Hospitals 99

Chapter 9 - Mr S 111

Chapter 10 - June...125

Chapter 11 - Waiting Rooms....................................137

Chapter 12 - Mr W 145

Chapter 13 - Mr L...153

Chapter 14 - The End 167

References 179

FOREWORD

Deftly weaving together stories from his career as a social worker and his personal life, Richard Wills has created a memoir that is strengthened by its duality. *Bloody Social Worker* is both an intimate and compassionate meditation on the lives of our most vulnerable and a robust work of social criticism.

Wills focuses on the service users he met and worked with during his time in social care. Their everyday lives are sketched with dignity and grace. The ones he cared for are shown as fully-realised individuals with vibrant internal worlds, which is a welcome change from the usual flat and dehumanising presentation of people with illness as statistics in the media. *Bloody Social Worker* is wonderfully human, and Wills' dark humour helps the reader reconcile some of the tougher aspects of the book.

On a personal note, as someone with a disability, I am indebted to the health and social care workers who care for me now, and who did so during my most acutely ill times. I would not be here without them. Their service is immeasurable and it is maddening that they aren't treated with the respect they deserve. Our health and social care professionals work in the most challenging environments while having to 'make do' on limited resources in times of increasing austerity. As Richard Wills says, there must be change.

In *Bloody Social Worker*, Wills demonstrates that there are real alternatives to the current system, which is one that benefits neither the service users nor the workers. There are deep problems and structural rot that need to be addressed and removed. Power and wealth are hoarded by the few and it is the most vulnerable in our society who bear the brunt of this.

Bloody Social Worker is not, however, a pessimistic book. Even after a life of stress and burnout working in social care, there is a fire of optimism evident in Richard Wills' writing. Wills advocates for change and gives the reader the sense that though there is much work to be done, essential human values of cooperation, kindness and contribution will lead to a brighter future for all.

Jillian Halket (author of *Blade in the Shadow*),
22 August 2022

PREFACE

I am now in a position where I am faced with the decision of what to do when I grow up.

Since the age of 21, I have worked in various sectors of social care. 32 years in total. The last 16 of these I had the much-reviled job title of Social Worker. I have decided, however, that my life working in social care must come to an end.

With local councils in financial meltdown due to the costs incurred by the Coronavirus epidemic, this inevitably leads to cuts in essential services, or 'efficiency savings' as some managers slavishly call them. Social care work is underpaid, underfunded, and undervalued, yet I would argue that caring for others in need is surely the most important job in the world, is it not? As a result, the bulk of newcomers do not last long in these most vital of jobs; the average stretch for post-qualifying social workers a paltry three years. So, maybe I haven't done that badly.

The decision to leave the profession that has provided my livelihood (well, it paid the mortgage and bills) throughout my adult existence, and has been at the core of my identity during this period, will not change. I am burnt out.

Burn out and social work is hardly a novel combination; it is a partnership as familiar as roast beef and Yorkshire pudding, or in more recent times, government and sheer incompetence. The forms and symptoms of this condition are as varied as the individuals who suffer and survive them. My own experiences of depression and work-related anxiety are common in this profession though. I have been prescribed various anti-depressants and offered countless talking therapies and forms of support. Whether the little white pills work for me is debatable, but as I have been reliably informed by my loved ones and the people closest to me that I am a 'bloody nightmare' when not taking them, I have chosen to accept such prescribed medication in recent years.

Living through periods of depression in my own life has given me valuable insight and increased natural empathy for those suffering such difficulties. Unfortunately, this does not mean that I necessarily take the advice I give to others. Unlike possibly wiser people, such as my wife Natalie who works in a similar role, the last thing I want to do after a stressful day of work is talk about it. I'd rather talk about anything but work, preferably in a pub with likeminded avoidants, discussing the day's politics / sport / music instead - anything but bloody social work. This is not a coping strategy that I would advocate, and indeed is the antithesis of the advice I offer others in distress. Maybe it is this contradiction which has led in part to the situation I now find myself in.

I never had ambitions as a child to do this sort of work. I just sort of fell into it. I do not say this with regret, or in an attempt to disown the choices I have made (I have no regrets, as some French singer once said, and it sounded better when she said it - it being in French and therefore more profound), but it is not the impression most people have when they enquire about the motivation for my chosen profession. Comments are usually couched in phrases which infer that my role is a 'vocation', that I must be a 'people person', and that social work must be 'stressful' but ultimately 'rewarding'.

So, am I a 'people person'? Well, I much prefer cats and dogs actually. When colleagues and friends show me pictures of these,

I can gush with the best of them. Show me a picture of their baby and, I'm sorry, it just doesn't do it for me. I suspect this sentimentality towards pets, often preferring them to humans, is a more common trait among social workers than many would think. Or fess up to.

I remember the weekly meetings with the Oldham Mental Health Team during which new cases were discussed and, if possible, allocated to individual staff - usually those foolish enough to make eye contact with the manager. The most extreme forms of human misery, abuse and crisis are presented at these meetings. We, as social workers, become used to, if not hardened to such horrific circumstances. One such meeting described a person whose background included familial sexual abuse, untreated sexually-transmitted infection leading to long-term physical disability, homelessness and early-onset of psychotic symptoms. During a psychotic episode, however, the woman's dog was trapped in a door - slammed in response to voices inside her head persecuting her - and suffered a broken back. The howls of empathy for this poor dog from colleagues were almost deafening, amid repeated enquiries about the condition of the 'poor mite' and whether the RSPCA had been contacted. Little was said in relation to the 'poor woman', and she was allocated to the staff member who made eye contact with our manager.

Despite this sort of thing, I probably would describe myself as a 'people person' to an extent, but only with *some* people. I've always identified with those on the edges of mainstream society - the outsiders and survivors. My working life thus far was largely concerned with those who lead such difficult lives. This book is therefore about and dedicated to these people - the glorious, tragic, funny, and enchanting figures who have been central to me, and the life I have led so far. Without them, I would be a completely different person. In every sense they have shaped my core identity. I will miss them. But I will not miss the job.

I have described myself as being on the avoidant end of the spectrum, so why write a book about my working life now, having made a clean break from it? Well, this book is about the colourful characters and the extreme, often comical situations I found myself in, rather than the grinding routines and stressors of the job itself. It does not offer any practical tips on how to navigate the plethora of bureaucratic processes in order to complete even the simplest of tasks which provide support to those in need. There is no in-depth examination of the complexity and contradictions inherent in the legal context of care provision, or a critique of *Section 117 of the 1983 Mental Health Act*. More astute minds can untangle such a mess.

2020 was a virus-ridden arse of a year for many and 2021 has hardly been triumphantly better. The period has produced, to say the least, a lot in the way of tumultuous change. This is undoubtedly part of the reason for writing this book now and for my decision to end a 32-year career. I have also suffered bereavements recently; both of my parents have passed, and not long ago a childhood friend. The death of important figures does bring with it a new sense of perspective and the realisation of how short life is. Such context has provided the spur towards personal change.

As you may already have gathered, this book does not aim to be an academic text. There are enough of those. It is more of an edited highlights package, instead of the full live experience. You will learn about some of the realities of social care, rather than the theory of it. There is no balanced critique of anti-discriminatory practice, or how to implement its noble aims while working in a sector severely constrained by a lack of funding - mainly because I don't think that you can. However, I do explain in rudimentary fashion some of the essential terms and concepts needed for an understanding of the social care sector. Six of the fourteen chapters concentrate on the life of an individual together with the part I played. Others deal with seminal periods in my work life and the major characters central to these. All the people and some of the places are anonymised for reasons of confidentiality. The stories are not an objective report, but they are as accurate and truthful as they can be, dredged as they have been from the fragments of my memories.

The title, *Bloody Social Worker*, infers no disrespect to those who work in this profession. Rather, it reflects the largely negative way that social workers are portrayed in the media and perceived by the general public. Let's face it - it's not the most respected of professions, is it? Stereotypes of politically correct, do-gooding, naïve souls with dangly earrings - both men and women (and others...I was a social worker, after all) - dominate and often go unchallenged.

Part of the problem is that most have little idea of what we actually do. The profession is one of the most varied, and the social worker in Mental Health plays a very different role to those in Adoption or the Children and Families department. Now, I could refer to a social work textbook definition to find out what I have been doing for the last thirty-two years, but I think it's better if I attempt such a description myself.

In essence, social work attempts to provide access to means and resources, such as housing, benefits, and other services, in order to enable a person to function more independently. (Often these tasks are now subsumed under titles such as care coordinator or care manager.) This is in addition to more direct forms of support and care which are characteristic of many areas of social care work. That'll do for starters. I hope the following chapters provide a whistle-stop tour which illuminate these essential features, as well as entertain with some of my personal experiences in this varied and challenging sector. The chapters are chronological and begin with my own struggles with mental health as a troubled teenager.

The people I write about represent my experiences in various services as I endeavoured to support those with mental health problems, learning disabilities, and drug and alcohol dependency - both young and old citizens, across all racial and class divides. Many are the stigmatised and criminalised: the 'underclass', prostitutes, drug users and sex offenders. Read on if you want to further understand the lived realities beyond these headline titles. All are complex individuals who perplex and amuse. Many could be described as my favourites. As professionals we are not meant to have such things, however, I defy anyone working in such an emotionally demanding field to tell me that they do not have those whom they look back on with special affection.

When things go wrong, when people who should be cared for are neglected, when deaths occur which shouldn't, it is all too often the social worker in the coroner's court that is the subject of scathing headlines in the press. Contrast this with the hundreds of suicides - those denied benefits and left destitute. Is there similar accountability for these decisions which lead to needless deaths?

Those that are still with us, but struggling, deserve more understanding, respect and support than they currently receive. There is definitely more awareness about mental health issues in general now, but this has not translated into the political will to defend essential services for those in need. And time and again they are faced with another round of funding cuts leaving them more vulnerable, isolated, and powerless.

For those who still toil away in social care, trying to make a difference, I salute you.

Things absolutely need to change though.

— Richard Wills, 29 November 2021

Chapter 1 - Teenage Discord

It is the last Sunday of the Easter holidays before a new term at school. Ask any kid…these are the worst Sundays.

On this worst of Sundays, I take an overdose of any pills that I can get my hands on. As it turns out, the majority are my mother's hormone replacement tablets. The rest are a mixture of paracetamol and indigestion pills. I studiously chew these as advised on the box. They ironically help with the eventual consequences - the most extreme form of indigestion, vomiting up the noxious contents of my stomach, mainly in my bedroom, and later in hospital when I swallow a foul-tasting brown liquid designed for such purposes.

I lose consciousness until my local doctor sees me at home and gives his medical verdict that I have been a "very silly boy". Next, my head is on my mam's lap, her fingers anxious but gently tapping my head and stroking my hair - which is matted in puke and sweat - as my dad drives us to the West Cumberland Hospital in Whitehaven. He is agitated and seems angry; I don't know whether this is at me or the doctor. My gut erupts, and I think I've shat myself as well. That's it, a blank until morning.

I wake up on the Children's Ward and slowly observe my surroundings. I try to adjust to the enormity of what I've done and where I am. I'm not dead. I wish I was. I don't want to be here. I don't want to be *anywhere*.

I watch the nurses milling around from the vantage point of my pillow. One is bubbly and talkative, obviously a bit of a party girl, as she unselfconsciously regales her colleagues with various tales of her love life. One nurse is irritated by her constant chatter and diligently keeps on working while the others talk. She checks the forms that are lodged at the end of my bed, looks at me and - unlike the others - acknowledges my presence.

"Are you feeling okay, Richard?"

I nod and muster a weak smile.

"Would you like some breakfast, some cereal or something?"

"No, thank you."

I can't think of anything I'd like less. This is quite enough human contact for now and so I crawl back under the protection of the covers and sleep.

I don't really sleep much, but it feels easier just to shut my eyes and shut the world out. I notice Party Girl again at the foot of my bed. When it comes to the hierarchy of looks, she's near the top of the pile and receives much attention from the male staff on the ward. She reads my notes and gazes at me with a strange look that I can't decipher. Once again, she doesn't speak to me. I get the feeling that she doesn't like me. Maybe she thinks that having done this harm to myself I am less of a deserving patient than the other kids on the ward. Or maybe I just think that about myself.

I wake up again and two men are standing at the end of my bed. I don't know what time it is, or even what day, but I'm not at school so it can't all be bad. I see there's a discarded bowl of corn flakes in milk near another bed, so I guess it must be morning. The ward smells of a mixture of this and bleach.

"Hello, Richard. I'm Trevor and this is my colleague, Pete. We're social workers at the hospital here. How are you feeling now?"

"A bit tired." That is all I can think of by way of reply.

Trevor is a proper 70s throwback. He's dressed in a big collar, kipper tie and flared trousers. It's 1980 - no one wears flares, fer fucks sake! His hair is over-the-collar length, and he has a moustache and beard. He reminds me of a darker version of Noel Edmonds from Multi-Coloured Swap Shop.

"We've discussed your case, Richard. Let's see how you get on for the next day or two. We can review things at a later stage. I think this was a cry for help, wasn't it, Richard?"

I offer a weak nod of compliance in reply. So, I'm 'a case' now, am I? And it's all just 'a cry for help' is it? You could have asked me first. I'd have told you. I tried to kill myself. For good. Cry for help, my arse.

The kid opposite me on the ward is getting out of bed, helped by a nurse. He's pale and has no hair which looks weird because he's only about ten. He is connected to a bleeping machine by tubes and the nurse slowly pushes this behind him as he trundles along using some kind of Zimmer frame walker. He's going to the toilet which is straight opposite the ward. I hear the nurse helping him with instructions and reassurance. He must have had an accident because she's saying: "It doesn't matter" and "Don't worry". I feel sorry for him.

Another kid, about the same age as me, comes up to my bed.

He's in pyjamas, the top of which is open showing his pallid white chest and a new-looking burgundy scar across his stomach. He sees me looking at it and explains, "I've had my appendix out. What're you in here for?"

I mutter a quick "I dunno" and feign illness, and sleep and shuffle back into my safe space underneath the bed sheets. I really want to tell him to mind his own fuckin' business, but I don't. I never say what I'm thinking. I can't.

Anyway, he's here for a *real* reason. It's not his fault. Unlike me.

~ ~ ~

These memories are what are left in my mind from when I was a depressed thirteen-year-old lad. It's interesting when trying to retrieve events from this now distant past - what has stayed with me in an often-vivid fashion, and what is missing. During my stay in hospital, I'm sure my parents must have visited, but I'm unable to dredge any memory of this. Yet, I distinctly remember the sight and sweet, sickly smell of those discarded, soggy corn flakes and wonder whether this is linked to my dislike of morning cereals ever since.

Memories are often delivered to the conscious mind in strange, fragmented packages. There is no central narrative and timelines are awash with inconsistencies. It is laughable to me now, that only these pictures and events have been retained, and other stuff either buried or stored away in the recycle bin of my now, adult mind.

I have no memory of being seen by a doctor or psychiatrist while in hospital. It may have happened, but I don't remember it. There is also little left in the memory bank of the period post-discharge. However, I do recollect my feelings of shame and embarrassment; shame at what I put my parents through - guilty feelings reinforced by their reaction; embarrassment, because I still wanted everything buried and just kept to myself. I didn't know what the kids at school knew about it, but hoped it was nowhere near the full truth. I imagined the conversation if privy to the last few days…

"So, what tablets did you take then?"

"Mainly me mam's hormone replacement pills."

"Fuckin' 'ell! Have yer grown tits yet?"

~ ~ ~

So, why did I do it?

I have pondered this question, not least for the writing of this chapter, but I cannot quite put my finger on a singular, overriding reason as to why. In many ways, it was just the usual teenage triggers which lead to angst and depression, and then some more. At this point in my life, I simply couldn't talk to anyone - I couldn't be myself. I hadn't yet worked out what 'myself' was and if I did have any idea I struggled to negotiate the ways in which I could be that. I literally couldn't relate to anyone.

I certainly don't blame anyone else. I just didn't have the emotional intelligence or resilience, or ways to cope with the life that I was in. I can't really judge my parents - they did their best, but they didn't understand, and I couldn't explain or articulate how I felt. I literally did not have the vocabulary or confidence to do so.

We never had the warmest of relationships and couldn't be described as a huggy sort of family. But this was quite typical and mimicked other families that I saw around me. It was very much a product of its time and culture - norms, which later in life, I consciously rejected. As my dad memorably told me, I was always a weird one.

~ ~ ~

I am in my second year at Wyndham Comprehensive School in Egremont, West Cumbria (now West Lakes Academy). It's a big school with around fifteen hundred pupils, covering a large geographical area stretching fifteen miles. As far as I can gather - as much as any pupil can - it's a good school. (This was well before the days of derisory league tables narrowly focusing on academic achievements.) From the wonderful Headmaster to the mix of teaching staff, there are many caring and dedicated people faultless in their support and guidance.

Part of my problem is that physically I'm a late developer. At the tender age of thirteen I experience the frustration and embarrassment of desperately seeking the emergence of pubic hair when everyone else seems to have a full Afro down there! After the summer holidays I'm greeted by lurid images in the PE changing rooms - lads who have caterpillar-like growth on their top lips and have developed into brick shithouses, whereas I've just stretched out a bit. (Was this really my life, or a scene from Kes that I'm remembering?)

Overall, West Cumbria is a hard place, and I am anything but. It is a country area with a few villages and small towns. Sports-wise, if it's famous at all, then it is for rugby league and, historically, Cumberland wrestling in which my great grandfather was a champion. The biggest employer in the area is Windscale, rebranded in 1981 as Sellafield after reports of radioactive leaks into the surrounding countryside and Irish Sea. The majority of kids' parents that I know are employed there, unlike my own dad who is a woodwork and metalwork teacher at the school I attend. All these factors enhance my self-image as an outsider who doesn't fit in.

In many ways it is the familiar tale of the 'sensitive kid' and how he reacts to a masculine code of behaviour he can never live up to. Skinny, self-conscious kids have it hard everywhere. I cannot recall specific instances of being picked on or bullied; it happened, but not to a degree that meant it was an overriding factor in my suffering. I am just so painfully self-conscious that I hardly speak at all during this prepubescent stage and I hate myself and practically everything and everyone around me. Looking back, it's fortunate - what with such a mindset and circumstances - that I didn't become an infamous Columbine-style killer!

I am not one of those happy in their own company. I am shy and introverted, but I don't think this is my natural, baseline psychological state. I just don't have the ability to *join in* and be anything else at this time. I hear the school banter around me and try to think of witty replies, but I can't actually voice them because I don't think they'll be heard. I just don't know how to handle myself in the company of my peers. I am thoroughly pathetic, and I know it.

Worst of all, I am hopeless. The next four years, before I have the choice of leaving school, feel like decades and I cannot go on feeling like this for much longer. That is the truth of the matter. I just can't see any other way out. That's probably why I did what I did.

Forty years later, I'm not the same person. But I kind of…am.

When I think back, the same passions in life - music, politics, football - were there in my fledgling self; pop music the most evocative expression of the arts (and hearing certain songs still takes me back to the time and place where I first heard them). One of my favourite bands, Blondie, were top of the charts around this time with 'Call Me'. And it seemed to fill a void. Another song that brings those times flooding back is Genesis's 'Turn It On Again'. Just hearing the opening bars gives me a strange feeling in the pit of my stomach. The anxiety and hopelessness that I felt as a 13 year old is manifested in this physical sensation.

I recently watched the brilliant series 'Up' which has interviewed the same people every seven years from the age of seven until the present day, now aged sixty three. I remember watching this with my family in my early teenage years. There was one figure who I sadly identified with. At the age of seven, he'd been a happy young lad, filmed in black and white in Liverpool. By the age of twenty one, however, he was destitute, depressed and hopeless, living alone near a lake in the Highlands of Scotland. I remember my dad railing against this man's despondency, saying something along the lines of: "What do you expect, if you just give up? You've got to get on with life!" Whereas my mam and I had a bit more sympathy and understanding for his predicament. It's no wonder the series has resonated so much with me, then and now.

Thankfully, there is much in my early teenage self that I do not recognise now. I certainly do not catastrophize in the same way as I did back then. My adult perspective has taught me that however grave a situation may look or feel there are always ways to make it through and come out the other side. I'm still guilty of overthinking and being led too much by 'What ifs' which invariably point toward worst-case scenarios, but my working life (supporting others going through mental health crises) has undoubtedly helped me identify damaging and negative thought patterns.

Another way in which I'm different now is that I'm reasonably comfortable in my own skin and thoroughly enjoy socialising with others. Rather than fearing company, I now crave it, especially in February 2021 as I'm writing this. Like the rest of the country, I'm still enduring lockdown and enforced isolation. Hopefully, you're reading this during better times when the option of having a few drinks with some pals in the pub doesn't feel like a far-off dream.

I am now in touch with many of the kids that I knew at school, via social media, after a gap of 30-40 years. This has been a fascinating experience, entailing as it does negotiating the divide between what I was and who I am now. Although my experiences at school did improve, to the point that I actually quite enjoyed the sixth form, I just didn't have the confidence to be myself at thirteen, and I was still trying to find what this seemingly elusive 'myself' was.

Confidence is still an issue in my adult life and I have periods when I'm prone to depression. There have been times when I have shut out the world and sought the protection of my bed. In my twenties, I still regarded myself as socially awkward, and my attraction to drugs like speed was largely because of this as it certainly brings you out of yourself. Anecdotally, I have found that taking stimulants to improve social confidence is common. Such a groove was relatively short lived for me though as I later discovered that instead of giving me more aplomb in social situations it made me feel like a coiled spring.

It has been difficult to write this, not because it means so much to me, but rather because it means so very little now. It is not something I have particularly dwelled on (avoidant as I am) or even thought about for a long time. It was over forty years ago, after all. When I read this, it seems to offer a somewhat thin explanation for such a drastic act, but there really is nothing else I can say, especially to those who know me but had no knowledge of this part of my life. The truth is that taking pills (and trying to take my life in the process) now feels like a very immature act.

Another harsh truth is that I probably would not have written this if my parents were still alive. We did not have a close or harmonious relationship and there was no adult discussion about this period of my life. It was not a conversation that any of us wanted to have. I realise this sounds almost callous, as though their death has provided me with a form of release or acted as a catalyst, but it is the truth as I see it, however sad and regrettable that may sound.

I write this not to compare my own experiences with those I have worked with since. My problems come nowhere near the issues I have witnessed in others in terms of depth or endurance. Rather, it is because I have spent a career wanting others to open up to me, so I thought I would show the courtesy of being a little more open back. Payback if you like. This early chapter of my life also gave me my first contact with a social worker, although it was hardly an inspiring one.

Despite ongoing depressive thoughts, my teenage life improved, but I was still a shy and awkward youth. I needed to escape my environment to develop any confidence, any semblance of a self where I could negotiate life on my terms. I needed to start anew. I needed the anonymity that a big city could give me. After studying in Liverpool, I therefore moved to Manchester.

Chapter 2 - Cedarmount Elderly Persons Home

Escaping to a big city worked for me and I enjoyed my years as a college student in Liverpool. It wasn't an instant transformation, but my self-confidence slowly improved while studying Social Science. I enjoyed the subject and mixed with people who were likeminded. The world of girlfriends, gigs and nights on the town opened up for me, and I was a more than willing participant.

I'd arrived, but student life couldn't go on forever and the time had come to enter the scary world of work. Liverpool wasn't known for an abundance of jobs in the 80s and so when friends from college suggested moving to Manchester, I joined them.

In the summer of 1989, I got a job as a care assistant at Cedarmount EPH - a council run residential home. Later that year I moved into a flat in Hulme, Manchester, situated a hundred yards or so from the home. Very handy! The home was purpose-built accommodation beside The Junction Pub and straight opposite one of Hulme's notorious and brutalist deck-access crescents.

My first encounter with Hulme had come a couple of years earlier while I was still a student in Liverpool. The earnest, politically conscious, and insufferably 'right on' among the student body at Edge Hill College, Ormskirk, made regular trips to Hulme for demonstrations in support of Viraj Mendis. He was a Sri Lankan national seeking asylum, protesting against deportation back to his home country, by claiming the right of sanctuary at the Church of the Ascension in Hulme. Mr Mendis had escaped the civil war in Sri Lanka, was a supporter of the underground rebel group, the Tamil Tigers, and feared persecution and potential death if deported back.

On the morning of 18th January, 1989, this was indeed to be his fate. Greater Manchester Police, then ruled by a thoroughly vile psychopath, Chief Inspector James Anderton, [i] raided the church, arrested Mendis and put him on a plane to Sri Lanka. Mendis later escaped to Germany where he still resides and became chairperson of the International Human Rights Association in Bremen. Because I knew people at the Church of the Ascension, I was later entrusted to look after Viraj's cat following his deportation. This lovely little tabby, who I named Scat Cat (because she was 'scatty as hell' in her early days), lived with me for ten years before sadly succumbing to a brain tumour.

All of this is true - fact. What isn't, and is indeed fake news, was what a friend mistakenly went around telling various people, that I was actually living with "Salman Rushdie's cat". Apart from Viraj Mendis and Salman Rushdie sharing four syllable names, there is no other known link between these gentlemen.

My first impression of Hulme, while still a student, was of the forbidding and decaying architecture, long neglected and covered in graffiti, and to be honest I found it downright intimidating. My initial reaction was, quite bluntly, "I can't live there!" It was only by getting to know others who resided there, and visiting regularly, that I discovered the vibrant culture of Hulme beyond its grim façade. It was then, only a couple of years after I initially dismissed the place, that I moved in to a flat on Scarth Walk with two friends.

The main attraction was the vibrant, local music scene. Many of my favourite indie bands of the time, Dub Sex, Yargo, King of the Slums, Easterhouse, among others, all hailed from this area of the city. This was also the time that the Manchester music scene was propelled to the absolute centre of the musical universe. The 'Madchester' era saw bands like the Happy Mondays and The Stone Roses leave all others in their wake, and they were part of the coolest, most happening club scene in the world. To be situated in the beating heart of Manchester was exciting for me - a musically-obsessed young man, educated by the late, lamented radio DJ, John Peel.

The only drawback was that the associated, nefarious activities and night-time clubbing were interrupted by a need to fund them by working for a living. Combining both worlds would become an ongoing challenge.

~ ~ ~

I was introduced to Cedarmount EPH and its residents by the assistant manager, who I soon found out was nicknamed Hindley by the other staff (more about her later). She took me through the various areas and told me where the residents should be sitting i.e. whether they ought to be in 'High Dependency' or 'Low Dependency' lounges. I kid you not! Most residents were living through various stages of dementia and the main part of my job was making their experience of life (in their twilight years) as comfortable as possible.

Some rudimentary on the job training was also given in regard to the essential tasks of lifting and toileting residents, and the upkeep of their rooms, bed making etc. Nothing could quite prepare me for the task of lifting people who were twice my body weight, transferring them from their wheelchair to the toilet for instance - me being a skinny 'eight stone in the rain' at this point.

The training included 'How to do a fireman's lift', which I

practised with my new colleagues. Despite being vastly more experienced than me, the exercise still elicited embarrassed giggles as I roughly manhandled them in a clumsy attempt to get a firm grip. Quite an introduction! Although there was guidance that this should be done with the assistance of a colleague, I soon found out that in practice staffing levels didn't allow such 'luxury'. Being new to the job I was reluctant to act alone, however, and so often waited for a colleague while in the toilet with the resident (adding to my feeling of inadequacy and sometimes stirring the resident's impatience).

On one occasion a resident, Mr Y, became lodged on the edge of the toilet as I attempted to transfer him back to his wheelchair, but had to shout for help. My embarrassment was assuaged somewhat by being told by my lovely colleague, Abbie, that this was a regular occurrence even with two people on hand. Mr Y looked far from impressed though.

My lifting skills did improve over time, and I soon learnt that it was more about technique and confidence rather than sheer strength. I handled most of the residents on my own shortly after without too much of a problem. Despite this, I always felt that we shouldn't be lifting people on our own for health and safety reasons, but felt pressured to do the same as my more experienced colleagues. It is no wonder that so many staff retire with back problems.

The job of a care assistant is not a glamorous one. Physical assistance in relation to every basic natural function involves contact with all the major bodily fluids. It does feel daunting at first - the initial wiping of another person's bottom something you get through because you have to. I always felt for the person in front of me. I know it must feel pretty awful and demeaning to have your bum wiped by someone else. Empathy for others' feelings is a prerequisite for doing this job in a sensitive fashion. This obviously became easier the more I got to know the occupants as individuals rather than the impersonal idea of 'residents'. The characters I became acquainted with and the snippets of their life histories were fascinating to the point of being overwhelming. And at this early point in my career, I found it hard not to want to talk about my experiences after a shift. Fortunately, I was able to get the many encounters and ordeals out of my system via my flat mate, Sarah, who was also working at Cedarmount.

We all have our own way of coping with extremes. Many of my fellow care assistants used the term 'tish' instead of shit, as in "Mrs T's tished up again". I always hated this so-called euphemism, and it was a term that came to be loaded with foreboding, especially on a shift after bacon and cabbage was served for tea. My own way of dealing with the task of wiping bottoms was having a good natter with the person receiving my assistance, while internally singing '[Get] Into the Groove' by Madonna. Having carefully-honed toilet humour is a coping strategy employed by many in care work!

The sight of a male care assistant was quite a rare one. The vast majority of my colleagues were women, and this gender imbalance is still seen throughout the care sector. A consequence of this though was becoming a target for the sexual energies of one of the more randy and disinhibited residents, Mrs D. At last, I'd achieved a lifelong ambition - I was being objectified! At first there were saucy comments, but these soon accelerated into the lewd groping of my body (if I let it, or was unaware of her presence). I needed to have my wits about me as I entered the Low Dependency lounge! The most effective defence was the age-old strategy of running away; speed being my unequivocal advantage. This soon became a slapstick pantomime where other residents would shout, "She's behind you!" as I feigned fear and horror before taking off - exaggerated run included.

~ ~ ~

A regular and heart-warming sight throughout my time at Cedarmount was of two best friends, Mrs D and Mrs G, walking around the home together, arms linked. They were constantly chatting to each other, giggling away, making no sense whatsoever to anyone else. It was a profound example of love and friendship transcending the horrific illness of dementia though. And my first, brief conversation with Mrs D I still recall after all these years.

Me: "Hello, Mrs D."

Mrs D: "Elephants?" (With added, bemused expression.)

Surreal exchanges such as this were a regular occurrence. The majority of the residents were also hard of hearing, and it soon became automatic raising my voice at work. This new habit - noticed by friends outside of work - is one shared by many who work with elderly people. It is mainstream, accepted practice not to challenge delusional content communicated by those suffering from dementia, but rather to play along with their randomness as far as practically possible. Learning this helped me cope with my mother's dementia many years later. At the end of her life, she barely recognised me, and often mistook me for my father - sometimes making suggestions that no son should hear! I knew that trying to impose a shared, accepted reality on her wouldn't do any good and could potentially disturb her more than she already was. I therefore generally played along with things, using humour as much as possible.

One lady at Cedarmount, Mrs H, thought that she was the manager of the home, and she would gently, but with a matronly and thoroughly-assured authority, check on the staff's whereabouts. She would then tell us off for tasks not completed promptly and would check on the progress of other jobs. We went along with this and sometimes played up for comic effect.

Mrs H: "Has Deirdre cleaned those commodes yet, Richard?"

Me: "No. The last time I saw her she was outside having another fag. I'd have a word with her if I was you, Mrs H."

We were all Mrs H's confidantes, so to speak, and regularly dobbed each other in to her and got used to her reproaches for our supposed misdemeanours. The sad story behind this is that Mrs H *was* actually a manager at such a home a mere two years before this. She suffered from early onset Alzheimer's, meaning that the disease is more aggressive and progresses faster. And in Mrs H's case the symptoms intensified when she was assaulted in an attempted mugging, sustaining a head injury and frontal lobe damage, drastically affecting her memory. A heart-breaking story, indeed, and because we didn't challenge her and instead went along with her beliefs, she seemed happy enough - or at least didn't appear unduly distressed by her situation.

This was certainly not the case with other residents - some of whom bitterly resented having to reside at the home. I felt then, and still do, that such a reaction was entirely understandable. Residents were, after all, deprived of their liberty - something difficult to accept, particularly for those with a more independent streak. There were, however, residents - a minority - who could come and go as they pleased, but most were denied this freedom as it was in their 'best interests' due to the ensuing risks in the outside world. [ii]

I wouldn't say that residents going AWOL and escaping the confines of the home were regular occurrences, but nor were they rare. On one such occasion, a resident, Mrs P, was found to be missing and I was asked to look for her in the local district. After running around the nearby area like a headless chicken, I eventually found her in the pub next door. Despite her confused state, she seemed perfectly happy and full of smiles and laughter, probably because she had enjoyed a rare trip out (rather than through the relief of being found). The memory of her big, warm, gummy smile while she stared up at me - all four feet of her, unable to tolerate her false teeth at this stage of her life - is one that still makes me chuckle. The staff seemed totally unsurprised at the sight of an elderly lady shambling into the bar, dressed only in her nightie and cardigan, knickers nearly around her ankles, speaking in her own secret language. "I knew she was one of yours!" they said.

Another resident, Mrs F, was also in the pub, nursing her half pint of lager. I let on to Mrs F with a nod and a smile (she was one of the residents who was free to come and go), but received a stony-faced glare in response. She certainly didn't want to be associated with the home, and especially not with her severely-demented, fellow resident. She was a regular at the pub and the staff knew her well. And I never saw her worse for wear because of alcohol, which is probably more than she could say about me! I left her to it and escorted Mrs P back to the home - after asking permission to use the women's toilets to pull her knickers back up. I entirely understood Mrs F's dismissive response and thought that having a pint was a perfectly reasonable way of getting through the day whilst living in such a place.

Respecting others' rights to personal vices (as I hope they would respect mine) also got me on the right side of other residents, including Ken. Ken was a large, well-built gentleman who used to tarmac roads for a living. He was of Irish descent and spoke in a gentle, lilting voice which belied his size and reputation for violence. He used his walking stick to whip the legs of any unsuspecting staff walking by. So, it was always with some trepidation that I approached Ken, as a painful bruise was the inevitable outcome. After many of these 'assaults', I confided in a colleague about my frustration and was given some expert advice: "Get him a can of Guinness…he'll be right as rain with you."

It worked a treat! From then on, me and Ken were as thick as thieves with conspiratorial nods and winks, and I made regular trips to the local shop for his can of calm, bought using his personal funds which were hardly ever needed for anything else. Some may call this a carrot-and-stick approach; I call it whatever gets you through the day. Because of this pragmatic and non-judgmental approach, I was also introduced to the shady delights of the betting shop.

Gambling has never been one of my many vices and, up until this point, I had never set foot in a bookies. There were a couple of residents who were well versed with a 'flutter on the gee-gees' but weren't able to get to the bookies and so it became my job to deliver their bets to these smoky dens of iniquity - and collect the winnings, if need be. One of the residents who hired me for this task, Mr J, was otherwise largely uncommunicative. I had to completely revise my assessment of his mental capacity after witnessing his detailed calculation of a horse's chances - his mind as sharp as ever. His ability to calculate potential winnings was also spot on - this from a man who needed support dressing and cleaning himself in the morning. Old habits die hard!

My co-workers at the home were mainly strong, working-class women from the surrounding districts of Hulme and Moss Side, with around half being of Afro-Caribbean descent. What they must have thought of me, a naive, skinny 'student' from West Cumbria in his first proper job, complete with highfalutin, social science theoretical framework, I couldn't imagine! One good thing about being so skinny though is that others often have the idea that you're not eating enough; the resulting sympathy being generous gifts of food. And so it was that I was introduced to the heavenly delights of Afro-Caribbean food - including jerk chicken, curried goat, rice and peas, and dumplings; stuff which is still my favourite food to this day. This was a time years before such food entered the mainstream and was only available back then in takeaways/areas which had large black communities.

One such takeaway was the fabulous Sam Sams in Hulme. The chicken there was the best - the most delicious and succulent that I have ever tasted. The place also had the added attraction of being open in the early hours of the morning; perfect after a night out clubbing. The scene in Manchester at this time has now become the stuff of legend, to the point that I am heartily sick of hearing anecdotes about nights at the Hacienda, so I shall spare you mine. A good time was had - that's all you need to know. Other local venues included PSV, the one-time home of Factory Records, as well as the *unofficial* club on the top floor of Charles Barry Crescent, The Kitchen. The use of drugs at these venues is well known. The air at PSV was thick with cannabis smoke - enough to feel the benefit without the need to smoke your own. Alternative liveners included the vast amount of ecstasy and amphetamines available at the time. (I couldn't possibly comment regarding my own consumption, except to say that 'Roobarb and Custard' was a very popular cartoon and theme tune in clubs at the time, and reputedly a personal favourite of Manchester band, Doves.)

After one night out I did an early shift at Cedarmount without having slept. Considering this was the case, I was quite wide-eyed and talkative. In fact, the briskness of my bed making and cleaning was remarked upon and complimented that morning. This was rare, as the rapid completion of such tasks was not considered to be one of my strengths normally! What colleagues knew about my life outside of work is debatable, but one thing is for sure, they weren't naive. This became clear when I went out with them on our Christmas do. After a couple of hours in a local pub, talk turned to where to go next - the consensus being a 'Blues Party' in Moss Side. I had heard of these subterranean events, but had little idea of what they really entailed. Nonetheless, I was up for anything at this time. The reputation of Moss Side was the stuff of national press headlines, with gang warfare and gun crime courtesy of the Gooch Close Gang.

I was led to a house around the corner on the Princess Park estate. It had a booming sound system installed and those present mingled in the darkness. The smell of weed was unmistakable, and as my eyes acclimatised to the lack of light, I soon realised that I was possibly the only white face there. Without my colleagues, who introduced me to everyone, I would have felt at best uncomfortable, but the night passed by in a perfectly enjoyable way void of incident. The sight of my older, female colleagues indulging in various illicit activities was also an eye-opener.

These were new experiences - all part of being young and starting off in life. By way of contrast, my job meant caring for people during the last stages of their life - sometimes the *very* last. Dealing with death was an undeniably hard, but essential part of the job. I was thus glad when handling my first dead body that one of my most trusted colleagues, Deirdre, took me through the various tasks in a sensitive and kind fashion. She tutored me on how to prepare a body before it's transported to the funeral parlour; washing it and plugging orifices. Involuntary bursts of wind can escape when a body is moved, which is always a disconcerting experience, and especially unnerving for a novice like myself. Most importantly, Deirdre treated the person in death as she would have done in life - talking to her as she moved and washed her. This is as profound a spiritual lesson as I have ever experienced, and I shall forever be indebted to Deirdre for this.

Observing the death of others can make us aware of our own mortality. I can't really say that this was the case for me as there was no epiphany, but such an experience certainly came later in life when I faced the death of those close to me.

Later in my time at the home, we lost one of our big characters - Mrs S. She finally passed about three months after it was announced by the visiting medical staff that she was in the final stages of her life. She was well known in the area for being a white witch and was reputed to have mystical powers that she could use at will. While washing her body post-death, I found a tattered piece of paper by the side of her bed. On it was a scrawled message which has stayed with me ever since.

"Whoever nicked my bottom set of false teeth, your left leg will go to the devil".

Another of the 'celebrity' residents living in Cedarmount at this time was a gentleman who only ever answered to the name 'Doc'.[iii] Before Doc arrived at Cedarmount, he was the proprietor of a dolls' hospital on London Road, near Piccadilly Station in Manchester. I had never heard of such a thing, but was assured by colleagues that it was a well-known place where parents took their children's dolls to be fixed. Some told me about their visits there - being scared witless by the ghoulish sight of hundreds of dislocated heads, limbs and bodies lay around a small, cheerless room. It was only through the words of others that I learnt of Doc's personal history; how he was at a late stage of his journey through the ever-increasing circles of dementia's footprint - unable to construct or vocalise sentences that could be understood.

This was the case with many residents, and it was frustrating only having partial pictures of them as they presented now. I heard about something called 'Reminiscence Therapy' and contacted a friend in Hulme who had experience putting this into practice. She took me through the basics - assembling a group, introducing a subject, asking about memories relating to it and coaxing them to talk. Simple! The basic idea: the more the memory is stimulated, the better it works. And I can vouch for the central tenets of this through my experience of writing this book. I decided to take the idea of trying to set something up (with residents who had the capacity) to the Cedarmount manager and, fortunately, she was supportive.

This was, of course, a far more difficult venture in practice than it was in theory. And the fact that I was a mere novice with little or next to no training or support didn't help. There was limited and often grudging assistance from fellow staff and management as my 'pioneering' therapy was seen as disruptive to the normal afternoon routine consisting of cups of tea and wall-to-wall residents forcibly transfixed by a TV that outlasted them all. Often, discussion - when it did take place - veered off into memories regarding famous people (including the Royal Family), rather than their own personal recollections or feelings about events. I had facilitated two or three of these sessions when one of the ladies present started disclosing some frank emotions about her husband who was killed in the Second World War. She told us that she'd always felt guilty about hardly grieving because, as she put it, "He was a right bastard to me and the kids".

Such disclosure obviously needed to be handled and followed up with sensitivity. At this juncture, though, a particularly hated matriarchal assistant manager at the home (known as Hindley for reasons I can't possibly go into) burst into the room without even knocking. She asked why Room 4 was not yet prepared for a resident that was due to move in that evening. I replied that I would carry out such a task after the session, but she was having none of it - it had to be done immediately. I apologised to all those present and saw the WWII lady afterwards to check that she was OK. Recalling such fraught, emotional memories and no doubt talking about them for the first time in decades had been brave.

This wasn't the first time that the priorities of those running the home clashed with my madcap, liberal, progressive ideas…like 'talking to the residents'. My run-ins with Hindley thus became increasingly irritating. Here was someone who seemingly modelled herself on Margaret Thatcher and Mary Whitehouse, with full twin set and pearls in tow. She was the only person in the country who supported the poll tax, and the only staff member not to contribute to the Ambulance Workers' strike fund in their dispute that year. Also on the list of her heinous crimes (which live long in the memory) was the time during a pre-work morning brew when she complained about the amount of tax she was paying, and subsequently got her pay slip out for all to see. Everyone at the table would have been earning no more than half or possibly a third of what Hindley was and so her actions stemmed from a complete lack of self-awareness, gloating, or possibly both.

Unfortunately, she was in control of supplies at the home and her stinginess was infamous. She acted as though the funds were coming straight from her own pocket. It was my job to shave the residents - men *and* women (no giggling please…facial only) - as I was deemed a skilled expert given my own clean-shaven, young man smoothness at this point. The home provided cheap, disposable Bic razors (other rubbish shaving products are available) for this task. Anyone who has ever used these knows that they are extremely difficult to wield without resulting nicks and cuts. And anyone who has undertaken such a task with elderly people, whose skin - especially around the neck area - is less elastic and can sag (combined with involuntary facial movements), will concur that the shaving room often ends up looking like an abattoir - or, in some cases, like the set of a slasher movie. I pleaded with Hindley to supply slightly more expensive, but ultimately far more practical razors, but to no avail. She was dismissive, telling me that this was due to a scarcity in local authority funds and that ultimately her hands were tied.

My internal reaction to this was "If only!" At this point in proceedings, I need to disclose my daydream fantasies concerning the punishment of despised workplace figures. Surely, I'm not the only person who has had thoughts about the best way of torturing their boss, am I? Well, for the more honest readers among you, I'd like to share one of my favourite theories. Namely, that I think medieval times cornered the market in punishment and make modern practices such as waterboarding seem tame by comparison. My preferred method is the classic 'Hung, drawn and quartered' with the added attraction of hungry rats nibbling away at the person's intestines, whilst they're still conscious, so to experience the lovely sight and associated pain of Roland's every mouthful.

Anyway, I digress. Matters had come to a head, the Reminiscence Therapy episode was the final straw and I decided it was time to start looking for a different job. I wanted something which gave me more independence and also more input into the lives of those in my care. I was eventually successful and offered a post in a unit supporting young people with learning disabilities who were 'challenging' in their behaviour.

This next chapter of my life reminded me of the truth behind the old adage 'Be careful what you wish for'.

Chapter 3 - Denton Road

People often say that first impressions count. I rang the doorbell at Denton Road on my first morning at work and was greeted by a young man around the same age, in his early twenties. After introducing myself, he told me his name and led me down the corridor, and then, unforgettably, asked, "You got dirty knickers on, Richard?"

After a bemused moment whereupon I questioned my choice of underwear, I was rescued by a staff member who escorted Mick back to his flat. He explained - rolling his eyes - that the resident, Mick, had somehow gained access to pornographic material, resulting in him being 'overstimulated', hence the bizarre introduction. Similar introductions were had with everyone Mick met and it was with some relief that I discovered I wasn't the only person being singled out for such intimate questions!

After this unusual breaking of the ice, I was shown around the rather bare and stark Denton Road flats and introduced to staff and residents; only a few, as most were at the day centre which they attended during the week. The whole experience became a little less daunting after bumping into an old Cedarmount colleague, Paul, now working at Denton.

We chatted and - sharing my interest in music - he enthused about how the site on which Denton Road was built was previously a 1960s BBC TV studio. It was in this very place that George Best, in his mod haircut pomp in 1965, grooved to the sounds of The Rolling Stones as part of the Top of the Pops audience.

This was one of the lighter recollections/moments in what would be a gruelling, fraught and, at times, bloody frightening first few weeks. The atmosphere of stress and tension seemed to seep through the walls, leaving everyone - especially newcomers - permanently on edge. What was clear is that the description of young people with challenging behaviour was left deliberately vague during the application and interview process. My limited understanding was of residents challenging institutional rules and routines, rather than the reality: episodes of violence, resulting in bodily harm.

~ ~ ~

It's my second week at Denton Road. As I enter a flat, I am warned by staff member Tom that resident Callum's mood has been building up all morning and is about to blow. I can hear him in his bedroom making strange, high-pitched noises. I am told to keep an eye on him, but only from a safe distance. Sean, another member of staff, joins us and inadvertently crosses Callum's path as he walks in. He is met with a square punch to his jaw. Tom and I drag Sean out of harm's way and an ambulance is called. He is out cold. Meanwhile, Callum trashes everything he can get his hands on in the flat. The television, plant pots, pictures and a table are all propelled at high velocity towards walls and windows - crashing down in the form of wreckage on the carpet. We hear the remaining fragments of his rage from behind the fire door and wait until his mood subsides before we enter again to clear up the mess.

Two weeks later, Sean bravely appears back at work, minus a front tooth. He is greeted by resident, Mike, who chillingly asks, "You been visited by the tooth fairy, Sean?"

Mike spends the rest of the day asking everyone the same

question.

~ ~ ~

I'm just into my second month. Resident, Mark, has just erupted. Everything in his flat is broken and bent - left as debris. The curtains and floor tiles are ripped and sodden with unknown substances. This incident is typical of many. Staff member Dianne and I are attempting the great clear up, while Mark crouches on the stairs, rhythmically stroking his top lip and rocking against the wall. I pick up a cup which is slowly leaking its contents. I try to lift the mood and ask Dianne, "Where's my pissin' mug gone?"

We laugh together in a way that borders on hysteria. And we both agree - there *must* be better jobs than this.

As I enter the Denton front door, I hear raised voices down the corridor. I walk past the main office and identify the voices as Mr O, our beleaguered manager and Tracey, a fellow support worker. They are at it full tilt - shouting at a volume where there's no need to eavesdrop. I retreat to one of the flats and hear snippets: "It can't go on"; "No one has a fuckin' clue what to do"; "What do you *want* me to do? I've tried..."; "What the hell do they expect?"

I don't know exactly what they're talking about, but I also kind of do. I can tell this wasn't a point-scoring exercise or a clash of personalities, but instead a venting of sheer frustration. Tracey leaves the office and is consoled by her colleagues before departing, barely holding back the tears. I never see her again at Denton.

~ ~ ~

These episodes of violence and destruction were not premeditated, but rather the product of placing together highly complex, damaged young people with behavioural problems resulting from profound, autistic disorders. And such conduct would now be described as 'meltdowns', 'blows' or - less professionally – 'kicking off'. One huge consequence of it was staff going off sick due to stress and/or physical injury, which inevitably made the job harder for those that remained. Core staff did their best, but were often at their wits' end, with little in the way of guidance and support.

As a new starter, I felt like I'd walked into a place in meltdown and so was pretty much instantly looking at alternative employment options.

~ ~ ~

Denton Road was divided into three flats, each housing two to four residents - some living there permanently, some on a regular-respite basis. I soon became familiar with the different atmospheres in each flat, depending on the individuals who lived and worked there.

Initially, I adjusted to the pace of the new job which was very different to my previous role at Cedarmount (constantly on my feet, multi-tasking as briskly as possible). The emphasis here was on trying to create an atmosphere as calm as possible, avoiding sensory overload and changes in routine which potentially acted as triggers to outbursts of anger. The job, therefore, involved periods of doing very little, apart from trying to read and anticipate residents' behaviour in order to mitigate such flashpoints and create a safe space. In football terms, this is similar to the role of the goalkeeper, rather than that of the busy, central midfielder; in other words, gluts of frenetic activity in response to crises, as opposed to constant motion. One resident's meltdown was often sufficient to destabilise another's routine which had the effect of toppling different lives in the manner of poisoned dominoes. Such situations were random occurrences, but always seemed to happen in twos or threes. Those who regularly travel by bus will recognise this pattern through bitter experience.

Kath was a young resident - in her late teens when I first met her. Many, including myself, were fooled by her small stature, big smile, and self-comforting habit of sucking her thumb, yet this was a young lady who could fight. She was well-practised in her moves and coped admirably with our basic restraining strategies. The most lethal weapon of choice in her armoury was the backward head butt, aimed with great force and speed so to maximise the victim's split lip or busted nose. I managed to escape such injuries while working with her, but there were many times when a less fortunate outcome came worryingly close.

Kath was intensely likeable, despite this - especially when she was distracted by activities which allowed her mind to steer around the anxiety that disrupted her mood. Once on an even keel, she was a joy to work with. And as long as tasks were presented to her in a calm and quiet manner, she was motivated to learn and took great pleasure in her achievements.

I supported her with daily tasks such as cooking a simple meal, but if it were left to her she would have lived on a diet consisting solely of that modern culinary classic, the fish finger butty. She was also especially happy when engrossed in her favourite artistic activity - painting; creating splashes of colour that Jackson Pollock would have sold for thousands.

Like many on the autistic spectrum, she was most comfortable in a structured routine with clear expectations and simple, understandable goals. Unfortunately, in a similar fashion to those on the teenage/young person spectrum, she was also resistant to cleaning up after herself or making her bed. In addition, her mood and behaviour were often upset by the hormonal imbalance of her menstrual cycle, rendering her practically impossible to work with when she was premenstrual, despite medication.

Aggressive outbursts tended to occur when Kath was asked to take part in an activity which she preferred to avoid - especially those outside of her usual daily routine. The weekly shop for groceries was often a flashpoint - something that we had to plan in advance to cope with potential flare-ups.

On one such occasion a colleague and I were out with Kath in Rusholme, close to her flat in Moss Side. She became impatient and started to exhibit early warning signs such as involuntary body movements and vocal twitches. We finished shopping as soon as we could, but on the way back she became irritable and started hitting us. A Police car drove past and stopped - the driver's curiosity piqued by the sight of two young white males coaxing an even younger black female, seemingly against her will, to walk with them alongside a road in Moss Side. It didn't help that ID wasn't compulsory in those days as it is now, and that we didn't have any paperwork on us. When the officer asked what was going on, we explained the situation as best we could and told him about our job. Unforgettably, he replied, "You don't look like social workers!"

This was not the time or place to question the validity of his observation with a smart-arse reply, although "Thank fuck for that!" did spring to mind, and we gave the officer our manager's name and number in order to check our identities and the rationale for this dubious looking activity. It was Kath herself who took control and literally dragged us away, obviously tired of the interlude and wanting to get home. The interruption strangely tempered her increasing anxiety, and she was quiet and subdued for the rest of the evening. I don't recall whether there were any repercussions, or indeed whether the officer even rang the office to verify our story. With hindsight, if he didn't, it was lax to the point of negligence, considering the potential for exploitation.

My memory of the support Kath received from Psychiatry and Clinical Psychology departments is mixed. At one consultation with a psychiatrist, during which Kath ignored him and distracted herself by playing with toys, this greying expert of the mind - dressed in a plaid, check three-piece suit, complete with dicky bow - described her as 'subnormal'. Noticing my quizzical expression, he attempted to qualify the 'diagnostic' term, stating that it was "a traditional" description, but…"we know what we mean!" I would not have struggled to know what he meant if had used the terms 'imbecile' or 'simpleton' either. Not wishing to enhance his profession's (somewhat shaky) reputation, he compounded matters by insisting that some of Kath's excesses were modes of 'naughty' behaviour, at which point I also lost all interest.

Advice from a similar psychiatric relic suggested that we "blow into the nose" of a young man (also prone to aggressive outbursts) upon first noticing his behaviour about to erupt. My inner dialogue replied, "You start us off. Be my guest, mate. I'll just get out of the way…afford you some room. See you later."

This was in contrast to my blank, resigned face on show.

The predominant tool at the disposal of psychiatry when dealing with challenging behaviour was (and still is) increasing amounts of antipsychotic medication - the preferred brands being Mellaril and Largactil. A side effect of these, 'the shuffle' as it was known, was common among many of the residents that I worked with - typical symptoms including an unusually stiff gait, plus the dragging of one's feet when walking. [iv]

Now, I don't want to give the impression that I'm 'anti-psychiatry' - I'm not. I have met and worked with many good practitioners since. However, those that I had experience of up to this point - while working in the learning disability sector - were particularly awful, anachronistic, out of the ark, even then, thirty years ago.

In contrast, I recall the invaluable support I received from certain clinical psychologists. They used behaviour modification techniques, which involved assessing problem behaviour in order to find identifiable triggers and thus develop strategies to reduce their harmful effects. To prepare for this, we were asked to fill in ABC charts following incidents of aggressive behaviour; ABC standing for Antecedents, Behaviour and Consequences. As well as written reports, we had to provide pictorial evidence in the form of cartoons or diagrams to best illustrate such episodes.

At Denton Road there was a central kitchen for all the residents, which provided poor quality, institutional food that was both stodgy and lacking in any nutrition. In light of this, it was surprising that one of the triggers for violent outbursts was residents not being served their favourite dishes, or not having enough of the said dish. It was a source of much amusement among the staff when I depicted stick diagrams of a resident chucking a plate against a wall, or trying to slap me; speech bubbles bellowing, "Lemon meringue pie!" and - even more unfathomable considering its dried out and inedible content - "Lentil slice!"

The psychologists tutored us in a way which entailed using short, sharp, simple sentences and increased use of nonverbal gestures. These were simple, bite-sized instructions and demands that challenged my natural inclination to offer choice; the latter said to confuse and promote anxiety in those with profound forms of autism. It was counter-intuitive for me, and at first felt a bit cold - even authoritarian. But once I got used to it, I had to admit that it *did* produce favourable results in terms of reducing levels of frustration and meltdowns.

One of those who I worked with in this fashion at Denton Road was Ryan. He was prone to massive eruptions - tension-ridden violent blows in other words; throwing and trashing everything around him. The nature and degree of his deeply disturbed behaviour was too extreme to work with in his own flat (after Denton Road closed) and so he was transferred back to Calderstones Hospital, where he had spent much of his childhood. This was one of the larger institutions in Lancashire where attempts were made to resettle most of the patients into smaller-scale housing, as part of the Community Care policy.

Most of the time Ryan was withdrawn, in his own world, displaying repetitive, self-stimulating behaviour such as rocking, but also self-injurious behaviour - slapping and punching himself, rhythmic touching and bodily movements. When he did speak, it consisted of simple, needs-led requests, or bizarre words in his own language, often repeated continuously.

"Matta pallata. Matta pallata. What does Matta pallata mean, Richard?"

"Rouche, Rouche. Rouche. There's no such word as rouche is there, Richard?"

Ryan was highly sensitive when it came to anything taking place in his immediate environment. Other residents' disruptive behaviour gave rise to anxiety which built up in him to the point where he lost control and exploded in a fit of rage. To work with him I had to get on his wavelength, which was both intriguing and intense. I had to be calm and measured around him - reading his mood so to give him space when his anxiety increased. Recognising changes in mood can be complex. For example, sometimes smiles aren't manifestations of pleasure, but rather...grimaces (displeasure).

By this stage our team were a tight-knit bunch, both assertive and united, and used to arguing the toss with those in authority if need be. This did not bode well amid the highly defined, hierarchical context of the ward. I was one of those asked to work with Ryan for a short period while he was there. We were told by management that this was in the interests of consistency, and that we should work shifts solely with Ryan, supported by the Clinical Psychology Team.

Unfortunately, this arrangement soon broke down. The ward staff had their own way of working, with little regard for our approach. It soon became clear that we were expected to be part of a staff team working with other patients on the ward. And the contrast in approaches between our team and the ward staff could not have been starker. We swung from cringing at what we witnessed, to incredulity, as the all-male staff strutted around with their bulky sets of keys, on patrol, ready to 'pile on' (as they called it) if anyone needed their physical restraint techniques; 'craftsmanship' they openly practised on themselves. Whether this was meant to somehow impress us, or was because they simply relished getting a good, hard grip on each other, was unclear. Either way, this homoerotic display of masculine prowess left my colleague, who happened to be gay, as bemused as I was. His beautifully camp, one raised eyebrow expression, perfectly conveyed our shared disdain at such Neanderthal practice.

I remember remarking that if you swapped the staff culture of the ward with that of the most punitive prison, there'd be little difference. I didn't notice any female staff, and the autocratic hierarchy made the working atmosphere feel more like the armed forces than a nursing one. The overriding, guiding principle was control, not care. This arrangement was never going to last. I was there for a mere two shifts, plus sleep-in, before I asked to be transferred back to Manchester and civilisation as I knew it.

I must have made some kind of impression, as the next colleague drafted for a shift there - Jane - relayed a conversation that she'd had with the team leader on the ward. We never actually knew his official title - Sergeant Major was one of the more polite monikers that we gave him though. He detected that I was "hard work" and "one of them militants". Impressively, Jane replied, "Ooh, I'll tell him that. He'll be really chuffed!" Needless to say, I was.

I carried on working with Ryan once he was discharged from his short stay at Calderstones. There was no noticeable difference in his behaviour at first, but he did seem to benefit from being in a flat on his own without any disruption from other residents.

There were still periods of high tension, and intermittent meltdowns, but these were fewer in number than they had been.

One memory from this period was 'the worst excuse ever' in terms of being late for work - even if it was absolutely true. One particular morning, I dreamt that the alarm went off, and so got up (out of bed), got dressed, left the flat, caught the bus to my workplace and went in as normal. Then the phone rang and a colleague asked, "Where *are* you? You were meant to be here at eight."

"I am here!" I replied. "What're you on about? Eh? Oh, fuck!"

As the realisation dawned on me that I was still in my bedroom, plus the sheer panic of it being 9.30, all I could do was offer sheepish apologies and make my way into work. Again.

Although working with Ryan - ever mindful of his mood and trying to defuse his anxiety - was stressful and often intense, I soon learnt that I was better at this sort of work than helping other residents with different problems. For example, there were two people at Denton Road diagnosed as hyperkinetic - a disorder characterised by extreme hyperactivity, short attention span and impulsive behaviour. Tina was one of these.

On the go from the minute she woke up to the last vestiges of consciousness before sleep, she was quick, agile, and exceptionally good at grabbing anything left unguarded - most of which was shoved in her mouth. This included cigarettes - one of her favourite things to 'lift' - but she was a damn fine pickpocket too, so ventured beyond easy targets. Tina was treated with medication based on, or the derivative of, Amphetamine. However paradoxical and insane this sounds, such an approach was said to have a calming effect; and is, in fact, a common treatment for related disorders such as ADHD. I only worked a couple of shifts with Tina, but it was quite enough. I just didn't have the natural energy and alertness needed to work with someone like her. Had I been required to work with her on a long-term basis, then her medication may well have been too tempting, turning *me* into the pickpocket!

Dean, the other hyperkinetic resident, was also extremely lively and energetic. He spent hours running from one end of the courtyard at Denton Road to the other, slapping the wall each time he reached it - so much so that there were clear handprints on both walls from his exertions. It was a safe space to release some of his pent-up energy. However, on one occasion Dean escaped the confines of Denton Road and ran into the living room of a nearby house, just as the family were sitting down for Sunday dinner. It turned out that one member of the family was late coming down for their meal and so Dean occupied the empty seat and consumed the plate of food in front of him with great relish. The 'rescue party' of staff found the family in a state of bewilderment and disarray - a Sunday dinner they would never forget.

Working at Denton Road was one of the most formative experiences of my younger life. The residents were at the extreme end of the spectrum in terms of their condition and behaviour, and obviously needed people with special skill sets to work with them. It therefore came as no surprise that I met some brilliant, competent and infinitely patient practitioners there. It was due to these colleagues, and their support, that I managed to get through often harrowing experiences. What astonished me though was the way most of the staff were treated - and certainly not valued - by the powers that be in the local authority; the ramifications of which contributed to the strike in the spring of

1991.

Chapter 4 - Trade Union Work

I was brought up with Labour Party politics. Both my mam and dad were lifelong members, and I joined the party at the age of 15. I have clear memories of the political events which took place during my youth, especially the election of the much-hated Margaret Thatcher in 1979. My dad put his "Don't blame me, I voted Labour!" sticker on the back car windscreen soon after. The turmoil within the party subsequently, including the Tony Benn vs. Denis Healey election for Deputy Leader, has many parallels to present day divisions. These events and the later Miners' Strike of 1984-85 were the subject of much debate in our living room.

One of my earliest memories, at about seven years old, is of my dad in a bitter shouting match with my grandad who was a proud, working-class Tory. He had been a train driver during his working life, and they considered themselves the 'elite of the proletariat' and therefore a cut above other workers. In the car on the way back home from Carlisle, I asked why my grandad had "snitched on" his mates at school. This was met with incredulity by my parents, until I added, "Then why did you call him a class traitor?"

Local Labour Party members in Seascale, Cumbria, often came round, and heated debates would ensue, such is the way with comradely lefties. I started to form and proffer my own opinions during these exchanges, but I was hardly the most assertive at that age. One of the regular visitors was our neighbour, Mike, whose family were close friends of my own. We were regularly at each other's houses, and I often took their dogs - two gorgeous whippets - for walks and was bowled over, sometimes literally, by their sheer grace and speed. It was therefore a great shock to hear the news, later in life, that Mike was one of the June 2010 victims gunned down by Derrick Bird, a taxi driver from Whitehaven. Bird killed 12 people and injured 11 others in a senseless and brutal 'shooting spree' on a cool Wednesday morning in West Cumbria on the 2nd June. Michael Pike - Rest in Peace.[5]

Trade union membership, in whatever job I have been employed in, has always been automatic - the default position, the politics of which was in my blood. My first direct encounter with trade union activity - apart from with the National Union of Students (NUS) whilst at college - was when I started at Denton Road.

Within a couple of months of starting the job, the workforce (and I) were on strike - the result of long-running issues, namely unsafe staffing levels and working conditions in the unit. These issues could easily have come to a head at any point during the previous years, but coincidentally boiled over at the time I began work there. It was an indefinite, all-out strike that ended up lasting for five weeks in the spring of 1991. And I remember it as a long and bitterly fought affair.

I quickly found out that Denton Road was far from a happy place. Intensely expressed emotions were the order of the day - and that was just the staff. A union meeting was called soon after I started, with National and Local Government Officers' Association (NALGO) branch staff in attendance. It was obvious to them and to all present that the Denton team were in meltdown - very much at the end of their tether. And things could obviously not go on as they were.

The accommodation at Denton Road was split up into three separate units, with two to four young people living in each flat. The staff were unanimous in stating that they needed two bodies present - 'double cover' - or at least *access* to another member during times when all residents were present. This was due to the risk (and experience) of physical assault - the individual worker being more vulnerable on their own. Management's response was to state that this wasn't possible with the budgets available, or indeed practical due to a lack of available staff. The union's response was that this was a matter of health and safety for staff which the local authority, as employer, is legally responsible for. There was, therefore, an impasse, with no sign of anything changing. I learnt that this had been the case for well over a year, so options were now being discussed in relation to industrial action. Limited, one-day strikes had taken place previously, with little effect, so a majority now favoured a ballot for all-out, indefinite strike action. The same issues around staff safety were raised in meetings at a nearby day centre, Rhodes Place, and action was planned in conjunction with the staff members there.

And so it was that during the Easter of 1991 I found myself on strike! As a young leftie, I must admit that I found the prospect quite exciting. Such enthusiasm wasn't unanimously shared among colleagues though. For them, this was not a matter of choice, but of necessity. No worker chooses to go on strike lightly - it is an action of last resort. However, as a form of teambuilding, I don't think there are many better options. And it's certainly superior to the methods I have experienced since - especially those cringe fests which start with "Throw the ball to your colleague and say something positive about them". My suggestion for teambuilding, namely that we all "get pissed, drop an E and have a group hug" has sadly never been implemented.

Going on strike does foster the 'All in it together' spirit.[6] Solidarity is central, and mutual support networks must be built to sustain each other's resolve. Self-organisation was thus crucial, and we were reliant on our shop steward for his political nous and skills in public speaking. (The man in question, Paul, became a close friend, and was best man at my wedding years later, as I was at his.) We had a rota for keeping a presence and staying visible outside the home - although this wasn't a picket line as such, as we weren't preventing emergency staff (mainly agency) from going in. We spoke to as many staff groups and media outlets that would have us. This was important both in terms of raising the issues central to our dispute and in collecting funds for the strike. Discipline and organisation were critical in this respect, and conduct such as being late for the 'picket line' - as I was on the first day of the strike - was understandably frowned upon.

Speaking to the media - both local TV and radio - was largely left to NALGO branch officers and our shop steward, but we all had a go at public speaking in front of various staff teams and union gatherings. This came naturally to some more than others. I, personally, didn't mind doing it, but was a little reticent and nervous to begin with. It helped that there were clear health and safety issues that we were fighting for though, plus having the conviction that we were 100% right in taking such drastic action.

We soon had to gently discourage one of our highly intelligent, but eccentric colleagues, Eamonn, from speaking too much, however. He was losing audiences by going over their heads with his convoluted delivery describing the "byzantine complexities" of the dispute. He did gain kudos by writing 'The Stalinist School of Management' on the office door of the Director of Social Services though, after he/she refused our request to speak to him/her. We made a sharp exit after realising that he'd written this with a permanent marker.

Enthusiasm and commitment among those on strike did drift the longer it went on, and it was difficult to know how much support we had in the wider community and, ultimately, how we could succeed with our demand of increased staffing, which required greater funding. There were episodes that lifted morale, such as Niall Quinn - then a renowned striker at nearby Manchester City - stopping by to offer encouragement, but such high points were becoming scarcer. Inevitable differences of opinion came to the surface and led to splits and factions, both politically and personally. We tried to manage these differences through diplomacy and mediation - skills in a dispute just as important as the conviction that you're on the right side. I felt like a novice though compared to my more experienced colleagues and found it difficult to bridge the gaps that were forming.

Tensions and debate were present throughout the month-long stand-off, which centred around our mistrust of the leadership of the local NALGO branch. There were legitimate differences concerning the money collected by those of us on strike, courtesy of various speaking events and functions. From our viewpoint, we were the ones going out, speaking and doing the work, and so felt entitled to the funds that had been generated (certainly from a needs perspective). The union branch stated that the money should be placed in a central pot, however, and distributed according to the rules and regulations of the constitution - in line with legal requirements. The legitimacy of what we were doing - sharing it amongst members on strike - *was* dubious and would be unlawful now considering the draconian union laws which exist, but something about it also seemed fairer and necessarily expedient.

Negotiations between the union and management didn't produce anything solid in terms of agreeing future staffing levels, but rather vague promises about increased numbers being provided when required. After five weeks, money was the major issue behind our decision to bring the strike to an end. The differences among those on strike were largely characterised by the individual financial needs of those with children to feed and mortgages to pay, compared to single people such as myself (far too single for my liking) with less urgent needs. Like many disputes, there were no clear winners or losers, but I did feel we were stronger as a workforce for having taken such action. A social care team going on indefinite strike was a rare event then and I am proud to have been part of a team that stuck up for itself in extreme circumstances. I feel that we were entirely justified in what we did.

Throughout the dispute, senior management stuck to the line that Denton Road was due to close anyway under plans to replace it with a 'Community Care' network of supported houses. We welcomed this, but reiterated that staffing levels would have to be increased further, as employees in individual houses would be isolated, more so than at the Denton Road accommodation. This was recognised and there were vague reassurances that appropriate, safe staffing levels would be put in place. One of the NALGO branch officials helpfully told us that we would have to "Suck it and see".

At this stage, management were negotiating with staff representatives and were wary of implementing changes without the union's co-operation - recognition of the workforce's position of strength. The experience I gained during this dispute taught me the difference between management *consultation* and *negotiation*. In school playground terms, consultation is the big lad telling you "I'm going to kick your fuckin' head in and then bounce it off the goalposts". A negotiatory stance, on the other hand, may suspend the bullying - or at least spare the goalposts the impact of my skull. Fine lines maybe, but I prefer the latter.

The majority of residents at Denton Road moved into supported housing in the local community when Denton closed after the strike in 1991. And most of the workforce, including myself, continued to support them. Later, some of us were relocated to other schemes - breaking up the original group who'd been on strike. Many of us believed this action was instituted with the aim of diluting the strength of our 'unruly' and 'troublesome' workforce.

Some months later, when the shop steward, Paul, resigned from his post, I decided to throw my hat into the ring and stand for election. As it turned out, no one else stood, so I was duly elected for the age-old reason that no other fucker wanted the job. I was a union rep, and later an assistant branch secretary (a modern title for convenor) for NALGO, and then UNISON, for the next decade or so. My role included representing colleagues who were in trouble in their workplace for a variety of reasons - misdemeanours, disagreements, errors, violations and the like.

All members have a right to representation, but some test one's patience more than others. Advocating on behalf of those who had fallen foul of new, stringent 'Managing Attendance' policies took up increasing amounts of my time. At one extreme, I represented a colleague with a well-known reputation for weekend hedonism. He had phoned in sick on the Monday with 'dehydration'. (Mitigating circumstances such as being sold a 'dodgy pill' tending not to hold sway in such cases.) I told my colleague to expect little by way of mercy and that his best course of action would be to make a grovelling apology.

At the other end of the spectrum, I intervened to suspend a 'Sickness Monitoring' meeting involving a member of staff who was away from work because her husband was receiving end-of-life treatment for cancer of the oesophagus. Before the meeting, she was in a highly emotional state, telling me that her husband

- who she'd been married to for over twenty-five years - was close to death. I tried to reassure her that we would get this meeting over with as quickly and painlessly as possible. The manager, however, followed the policy script to the letter, making no allowance and showing no kind of sensitivity to this poor woman's circumstances, to the point of asking, "When do you think you'll be back in work on a normal, full-time basis?"

I asked for a break in proceedings. After speaking to the lady, I cornered the manager outside and asked him, while close to losing my rag, "What the hell do you expect her to say?! When he's safely snuffed it and buried?"

I suspended the meeting, reported the genius to his line manager and demanded an apology for the gross insensitivity shown. I also said that I would make this official, using the grievance procedure, if this was not forthcoming. An apology was given and the sickness procedure suspended indefinitely. I enjoyed being able to help this poor woman in her time of need, but most situations were not as clear cut.

I undertook training for the role of union rep through the further education college in Manchester, MANCATT, which was invaluable - as was advice from more experienced shop stewards and branch officers. We also had monthly stewards' meetings in each service sector where we could air our difficulties and swap news and advice. I learnt to keep an open mind when dealing with members' grievances and disciplinary proceedings as there are usually two sides to every story. One member bitterly complained about his line manager, whom he said was unfairly applying performance monitoring procedures and thereby questioning his competence. However, he neglected to mention this was a result of giving the wrong medication to residents on three separate occasions, and so I had to diplomatically state that such a measure was appropriate considering these recent mistakes.

I often felt that my work for the union was both thankless and unrecognised at times. On countless occasions I dealt with members' enquiries along the lines of "What's the union doing about this?" and tried to reframe such requests along the lines of "We're the union. I'm merely a representative. What do *you* want to do about it? What action are you and your colleagues prepared to take?" It is a truism that I learnt by experience and was often in a no-win situation when representing those at the devout end of the membership. If they won their case, the response was invariably, "Thanks be to God!" But if they lost, it was generally my fault! God was evidently on a cushy number when it came to job security.

After eight years as shop steward, I stood for election as assistant branch secretary within the union at Manchester City Council Social Services Department, and subsequently won. This inevitably involved contact with far-left groups often found on the margins of union activity. Individuals within these parties, who I'd previously had reasonable relationships with (prior to the vote), now - just days later - accused me of being co-opted by the branch establishment. I was, by implication, a "sell out" therefore. I had been aware that these 'parties' operated with a sectarian mindset, but this was the first time I'd been on the end of it. From that point on, I had a healthy mistrust of all their actions. And I have little doubt that in the unlikely circumstance of these groups gaining power, their whole edifice of solidarity would crumble within weeks amidst bitter infighting and recrimination.

In theory, this new post should have given me more time to devote to development matters within the branch, and a greater political role. In reality, the increased pace of change, regrading of job roles and redeployment, meant there was more 'bread and butter' disciplinary / grievance work, particularly with members that I did not know, leaving little time for anything else. My facility time - time allocated by the local authority for the union role - was two days a week, the rest of the time spent in my post as network support worker. On top of this, I had also started a part-time diploma in Social Work at Salford University which took up one night a week due to lectures and seminars. I certainly had my work cut out for me at this stage of my life.

The work for the union involved more meetings and negotiations with senior management in the social services department - usually accompanied by one of the full-time branch officers. These were largely constructive and meaningful meetings which at least showed willingness by management to negotiate and prepare the way with the union for any future changes they had in mind. We met with the head of the social services department, Mr K, in this capacity on a regular basis.

Mr K was a perfectly decent and affable man who, unfortunately, had a penchant for using the most clichéd management jargon imaginable. After a few meetings alongside the same branch officer, Sid, we devised a game to pass the time during these often laborious proceedings. We called it 'Management Lingo-Bingo' and it meant us predicting the choice phrases which would be aired, ticking them off as we went along in a thoroughly surreptitious manner. We each took notes during these meetings anyway, so it was easy enough to fill out separate bingo cards without those on the other side of the table detecting anything.

On the agenda today 21/08/99:
1) Regrading claim, new terms and conditions. 2) Ongoing

disciplinaries. 3) Sickness and absence procedures. 4) Grievance outcome. 5) AOB.

The atmosphere is tense, but convivial, as they get down to business…

"I think we need to be singing from the same hymn sheet on this."

Sid 1 Richard 1

Mr K's in there early with an all-time classic, easily predicted by both players.

"There's a flexible approach needed here."

Sid 2 Richard 1

Wily old campaigner, Sid, takes the lead anticipating this practically meaningless nonsense; novice Richard left in his wake.

"We need a sound, cost-benefit analysis to guide this."

Sid 3 Richard 1

School boy error from Richard, showing his inexperience. Textbook from Sid.

"We need to see the bigger picture here."

Sid 4 Richard 2

An easily foreseen, hoary old cliché from Mr K.

"We all need to be kept in the loop about this."

Sid 4 Richard 3

A rare mistake from Sid forgetting that piece of 'stating the completely obvious'. Richard clawing his way back.

"I think we need to draw a line in the sand here."

Sid comes in with a classic, union platitude of his own! This game really could go either...

And so it went on. Mr K delivered his missives with a warm, country farmer-like 'Gerrof moy laand!' accent which inevitably led to merciless, post-meeting mimicry by Sid and I. I don't recall either of us ever completing the bingo card, and there were no jubilant shouts of 'House' to my knowledge, but it helped us retain our sanity.

The issue of weekend working started to be raised regularly at meetings. Network support workers were on the rota for one weekend in two, but Mr K and management planned to change this to two weekends in three. Anyone who has worked weekend shifts knows the cost – missing family functions, birthday celebrations, football matches, normality. That and being asked by friends if you wanted to go out at the weekend and having to reply, "No, sorry, I'm working, but I'm free next Tuesday."

In light of the new management posts that had just been created, all of which were Monday to Friday (9 'til 5), we expressed our opposition. Negotiations reached an impasse and we informed Mr K of our intention to ballot our members over the issue and seek their views on potential industrial action. The ballot results indicated that the vast majority were in favour of taking strike action. A one-day strike by network support workers took place, but the outcome of this was, at best, mixed. There were pockets of unanimous action, but in far too many areas a minority of staff chose to ignore the strike ballot and go to work. There were even people who chose to take overtime in order to break the strike. How union branch colleagues and I referred to these people cannot be repeated in polite company.

We called off any plans for future action, in light of the mixed, staff response and had no choice but to accept the increased weekend hours. The reality of working with people who had broken the strike - the same ones who still asked, "What's the union doing about..." - started to become irritating.

Being pulled three ways - doing my support worker job, trade union work and social work course - started to take its toll. Something had to give. After much consideration and discussion with my partner at the time, Sue, I decided to resign from my job and the union position that went with it. The prevailing winds were (and still are) against public sector provision of services on this scale, and there was increased competition from the voluntary and private sector for its share of the public purse - all of which undercut the public sector in terms of wages and conditions. Looking back, Mr K and the management team's actions were understandable as - despite our opposition - they saw themselves as trying to protect these services in the context of tighter funding and increased competition.

Paradoxically, this situation, as well as leading to the conditions which prompted my eventual departure from the council, also provided me with opportunities to fund myself while studying. With the experience I had, I knew that I could get bank and agency work, and so for the next couple of years (before qualifying as a social worker) I spent time working in the voluntary sector.

~ ~ ~

Trade unions, as a whole, have had to adapt to new, more specialised forms of service delivery in social care as in the rest of the economy. Teams tend to be smaller, with their structure more complex; individual team members often working for different employers. There may also be agency workers and bank workers employed in the *same* workplace; many of the previous 'in house' support workers now replaced with personal assistants employed on a casualised, zero-hour basis. Outside individual teams, many services are now run by the private and voluntary sectors, with little or no history of trade union involvement. The challenges for unions in this increasingly fragmented, 'post-Fordism' world are thus huge, and the pace of change around us continues to accelerate.

Despite these ever-increasing challenges, trade union membership nationally has increased by over 200,000 since 2017. This increase is reflected locally, in Oldham, with new members coming from private sector care homes, reflecting the need for strong representation for those working on the frontline in the fight against Coronavirus and the many issues that exist. Trade unions are the biggest, voluntary organisations in the country. The vast majority of branch officers and representatives earn no extra money for the responsibilities that they take on - something that, in my experience, is not always understood by members. I believe that the need for union representation is greater now than ever, with far more employees - especially younger people - recruited in social care and beyond, often on casualised contracts which result in gross instability. Unless we think that job insecurity of this nature is inevitable and fair enough, then perhaps it is time to form those bonds within the workplace once more.

Chapter 5 - Mr M

Mr M was one of the funniest, most unique characters I had ever met. His raucous laugh was infectious, as was his wide, gushing smile. His daft sense of humour, foul language and wry take on life made being in his company a pleasure.

He lived in a staff-supported house with three other adults - in the Burnage area of Manchester. Five staff worked shifts on a rota basis, including sleep-ins. One of those, for eighteen months in the mid-to-late nineties, was me. We often worked on a single cover basis (on our own), but had the benefit of another staff member at certain times of the week for designated activities e.g. shopping, leisure pursuits.

I lived a short distance away in the neighbouring area of Levenshulme. I had recently bought a two-up, two-down terraced house - the deposit largely coming from the proceeds of a backdated regrading claim. We were now residential social workers and finally paid this settlement - an extra £1,500 - just before St Patrick's Day in 1996; a memorable day for me especially. After a lengthy day celebrating at Longsight Irish Club, I announced to friends that I was "going for a curry", but somehow stumbled instead into a moving taxi's windscreen, smashing it and leaving me with a dislocated collarbone, broken teeth, and scars to my chin and forehead. The first I knew of it was coming round in A&E at Manchester Royal Infirmary, to the worn out and somewhat disapproving looks of the overstretched nurses on duty. I'm sure I wasn't the only inebriated eejit they had to deal with that night, but all the same, it wasn't one of my proudest moments.

~ ~ ~

All four men in the Burnage house had been resettled from Calderstones, in Whalley, Lancashire - the large hospital institution where those with learning disabilities and/or mental health issues had lived, often the whole of their adult lives.[7] The majority of those resettled in Manchester under new Community Care legislation seemed to come from here.

Mr M was diagnosed with a learning disability known as Down's syndrome. He was in his fifties when I knew him - relatively old for someone with his condition; the average lifespan in 1983 being 25 years, but then in 2017 increasing to 60. This dramatic increase over such a short period of time has largely been attributed to ending the institutionalization of disabled people and the corresponding, inhumane practices associated with it.

Mr M had a wicked sense of humour and a name for each member of staff - some kinder than others. 'Fat Arse' he didn't have a great liking for, and neither did I, but I still had to correct him - without laughing - when he told me, in hysterics, about the washing machine flood and said staff member slipping "on her big, fat arse".

Another colleague was re-christened 'Mrs Miggins' - there being no obvious explanation for such a label. The woman in question was not the quaint-looking, olde Lancashire pie seller that such a name evoked. Mr M particularly liked one of the other female staff, though, on many levels. Chantale was mixed race and he named her 'Almonda', in recognition of her brown skin and exotic beauty; raised eyebrow and twinkle usually accompanying his old man flattery. (Some may understandably wince at such nicknames based on skin colour. All I will say is that there was certainly no malice involved…lechery perhaps, but no malice.) My name was Barry Richards, after a South

African cricket player from the 1970s. At other times he chose to call me 'Mytherin' Bastard' - a term he used in jest, although others may not have understood this when he introduced me in public this way.

Mr M's capacity for recalling obscure, cultural figures - usually from the 70s - knew no bounds, often displaying amazing feats of memory. He was especially knowledgeable about esoteric pop acts and liked to spend the afternoon listening to vintage radio channels (BBC Radio 2), calling out the act's name as soon as a tune came to him.

"Ay, Mytherin' Bastard - Boz Scaggs is on!"

"Oi, Barry - it's Gallagher and Lyle!"

He didn't bother with the less obscure acts. He knew we ought to know who Tina Charles was, after all! I apologise to anyone below the age of forty five reading this. Don't worry - only a small percentage of pop music pedants like myself will have heard of such delights. The important thing is, Mr M did.

His love of music was also evident at the monthly disco, held at a local club, catering for those with learning disabilities, and with their carers in tow. The style of dancing at these events was refreshing for its enthusiasm and sheer joy, even if lacking in technique and co-ordination. However, when Mr M took to the floor, everyone was aghast at his moves - gliding across the room with grace and aplomb. This man could moonwalk with the best of them - just one style among many from his considerable locker of groove. Problems only occurred when others rudely got in the way of this funkmeister's performance! One such figure was Mr T...who was blind. He lived with Mr M at the house in

Burnage, but they were not close - even at the best of times. When the inevitable happened and they collided on the dance floor (Mr T just as exuberant), this invariably led to violent clashes, and they had to be separated by staff.

Such displays of fluid and dexterous movement contrasted with the 'crippled by arthritis' role that Mr M played inside his home. The aim was seemingly to get staff to do tasks for him - tasks that he was perfectly capable of completing independently, but that new staff offered to do, taken in by his floundering, disabled act. If, during one of these performances, he miraculously discovered the strength to walk, he would then suddenly fall in theatrical fashion - akin to a Premiership footballer taking a dive in the penalty area. I became accustomed to these pantomime displays and would give them short shrift, despite his efforts (my favourite response being "Oh, Vic, I've fallen!" - a line from comedy duo, Reeves & Mortimer, which was popular at the time). I would sometimes dive to the floor alongside him and pretend to writhe around in pain, which usually had the desired effect of him breaking into laughter whilst issuing insults regarding my "pathetic" conduct.

"Barry! Gerrup, yer daft bastard!"

"You started it!"

Another regular routine was the smuggling of food in the middle of the night - items taken from the fridge and tucked down Mr M's trousers when he assumed everyone was asleep. He would then quietly retreat to his room and consume the spoils or store them for later. We tried telling him that such stealth wasn't necessary as the food was his anyway (freely available to everyone who lived there), but habits like this weren't uncommon to ex-Calderstones' residents or those similarly institutionalized; the stealing and guarding of food a survival strategy when up against strict and inhumane regimes. This behaviour was so ingrained that none of our reassurances altered it. And reserves of rotting bananas, defrosted, uncooked fish fingers and tubs of (now liquid) ice cream were often found amidst the debris of his room.

Another of Mr M's habits was to keep his clothes on, at night, in bed - possibly with these midnight raids in mind. He was never at his best in the morning - probably as a result of these nocturnal activities - and was certainly not a willing, early riser. Therefore, it wasn't with his usual, caustic cheer that he responded to my coaxing requests (mimicking and distorting Primal Scream's "Rocks"): "Get yer Socks off, Get yer Socks off, Honey". He may even have called me a w*nker, if my memory serves me right. As someone who could never be described as a morning person though, I thought it perfectly apt.

The role of staff was to support and "de-institutionalize" these men, reducing certain forms of habitual behaviour and helping them become more independent when it came to everyday tasks. Inevitably, there was a limit to this, and some tasks - especially cleaning - needed to be undertaken by staff to prevent the home environment turning into a hazardous "shit tip".

Each member of staff had their own way of working – generally informed or influenced by their own values and habits. And this sometimes led to tension and disagreements. A source of conflict would typically be the content of the weekly food shop. Although the idea was to support residents' preferences and choices (within reason), purchases tended to reflect the staff members own eating habits. I remember complaints about the number of vegetables being bought, as too many were going off.

"You could try cooking and eating them!" tended to be my response. At the other extreme, the Fairtrade organic quinoa was never a particular favourite of the residents or, I suspect, any honest and rational human being.

Mr M, as made clear, wasn't fussy or pernickety, and although he never seemed concerned about being overweight or becoming ill from the wrong type of food, something that *was* an issue was his capacity to break wind. The sheer voraciousness and volume of his farts and burps is unsurpassed; his thunderous output becoming such an everyday - or rather hourly - occurrence that no one thought anything of it. Well, apart from Mr M himself who looked mightily proud, announcing to everyone and no one, "Ooh, that was a big one!"

Although not a problem in the privacy of his own home - the neighbours being tolerant people - letting rip in public was a different matter. Mr M's natural calling card, the loud fart or burp, would often bring unwanted attention in public and had the potential for embarrassment or even disapproval. I was quite used to his greeting of a hug followed by a loud guff, but to the uninitiated – a shop assistant, for example - it could be mightily unsettling. Therefore, we tried to reinforce boundaries when around strangers. Although it curtailed his affectionate nature, the aim was to project a more 'positive image' in the community. That was the theory anyway, or rather a watered-down version of "Normalisation".[8]

The approach had its logical rationale: Mr M, indiscriminately hugging strangers, could result in complaints or - worst-case scenario - claims of abuse and exploitation. Therefore, trying to support him in becoming more 'boundaried' with strangers was appropriate. It did, however, irritate me a little, as it imposed arbitrary and value-laden standards of behaviour. I can't remember a single instance of someone reacting to Mr M in an especially negative way. He was well known and seemed to be well liked in the community. If the perception of him was "that little Down's syndrome guy who farts a lot" then was there really a problem?

There *were* times when Mr M's impulsive behaviour had to be reined in in the interests of safety. One such occasion was celebrating one of the men's birthdays by way of a helicopter ride over Blackpool. Events like this - going out, doing something pleasurable, meals out, or weekends away - became rarer as time went on, or as funding for the brave new world of community care dried up. These outings were far from commonplace, in other words, before you start thinking that we were living the life of Riley or doing the conga most days, funded by Mr & Mrs Taxpayer. It was everyone's first (and my last) time in a helicopter, so there was much excitement. Mr T, as described earlier, had a natural exuberance, and when excited didn't pause for breath – his non-stop talking something which always irritated Mr M. In the helicopter, high in the sky above the coast of Lancashire, the inevitable conflict came close to boiling point and - without staff intervention - could have led to a calamity.

Whilst Mr T was excited, talking endlessly to no one in particular, Mr M was shouting (lip-reading required as we were wearing noise-reducing headphones), "Shut the fuck up", "Tell him to fuck off, Richard", and then repeatedly, "Tw*t" and "W*nker" while kicking the seat in front of him where Mr T was sat. I reached over to calm down the potentially dangerous situation and divert Mr M's mind elsewhere. Thankfully, I was successful. There was no mid-air bust-up, and I'm not sure the pilot even noticed the disturbance, concentrating as he was on flying the helicopter.

~ ~ ~

Mr M had a close and loving relationship with his sister, Elizabeth, who visited him every weekend. She invariably brought magazines for him which he devoured with untold passion. They were 'Women's' magazines, which was all the better for Mr M who definitely liked looking at pictures of the female form. Whether his sister knew that it was the pictures he was drawn to, and that he had a perfectly functioning sex drive, was unclear. It is the case, in my experience, that families of people with learning disabilities can infantilise them, not recognising their perfectly normal, adult sexual impulses. They were certainly evident to the staff who worked with him - especially the females. Mr M became well known at the local newsagents for his love of glossy magazines, especially the "big 'uns" which he sought out (this related to the *thickness* of the magazine rather than anything else). I tried to steer him towards the then burgeoning Men's magazine section, led by Loaded and the like, which were a bit more appropriate at least and provided for his needs in a relatively safe fashion. Perhaps if he was taller – more than five feet in height - he may have spotted some of the top-shelf glossies which would have led to a whole new debate about appropriate purchases.

~ ~ ~

I worked in this job for around ten years. As time went on and funding became the determining force, the nature of the role changed and we became more like glorified housekeepers. The senior manager, Mr K, who I had contact with in my work for the union, demanded more 'flexibility' from the workforce and described the networks as 'a Rolls Royce' service. He was a man

– as previously noted - very much partial to management clichés. As staffing levels slowly eroded though, we were expected to cover many different houses during a shift, relying on agency staff to cover the ever-widening gaps in the rota.

It became clear that only a small minority of eligible people in the community actually received this service - many more still dependent on family and often isolated. Our services were, in hindsight, small pockets of progress, but part of an overall picture of needs not being met. Because of the nature of our work, we spent long periods of time with people, devoting much of our life to them, but sadly usually lost touch afterwards. This was the case with Mr M, and sadly I only found out that he had passed away when doing research for this chapter. While still living in Levenshulme, I inevitably saw him and his housemates occasionally, and always found such moments a pleasure. He remembered my name, without fail: "Ooh, look, it's Mytherin' Bastard." And the affectionate hug and compulsory fart were still as ferocious as his language.

Mr M lived to the grand old age of 74. He passed away in 2018. At the start of my life, that age would have been a record for someone with Down's syndrome, so is something I think we should all celebrate. Of all the chapters in this book, this was one of the easier and more enjoyable ones to write, as remembering him still makes me smile.

My interest in working in Learning Disability services had by then waned, and I was looking to expand my experience in other sectors of social care while studying to become a qualified social worker. I look back on my days in this service fondly, however. Fellow staff were, overall, a good bunch (many are still friends now) and I enjoyed a healthy social life spaced around shift work. The income was stable, as was my personal life - living with my long-term girlfriend, Sue. The service began increasingly concentrating on those with 'challenging behaviour' though - the sort of complex work which I'd had my fill of while at Denton Road - and so I needed a change.

I drastically reduced the hours in my present job and ventured into the arms of the voluntary sector, initially unpaid.

Chapter 6 - The Voluntary Sector

For the first time in my life, I resigned from a job. My stint working for the Learning Disability networks had come to an end. Even on reduced hours, I'd had enough, and so I completely bit the bullet. It was a scary time, especially financially, but I knew I'd made the right decision.

My first experience working in the voluntary sector - sometimes called the Third Sector - was at Lifeline Drugs Project. I started as a volunteer at the needle exchange based on Oldham Street in Manchester, at the heart of the Northern Quarter, a fast-developing area where much of the third sector was based. The Big Issue, Turning Point, Shelter and N'Gage all had offices and offered services in this part of the city. Much of the voluntary sector originated in the 1970s when they were trying to fill gaps in services as a result of public sector inertia. Manchester-based Lifeline, set up in 1971, exemplified this and ran services for those with a drug dependency; the people overseeing it very knowledgeable as they themselves had experienced issues with heroin addiction. Up until the 1990s this was a small-scale operation staffed largely by volunteers.

By the time I worked there, in the early 2000s, its services had expanded across the country, and the Lifeline 'brand' was on the cusp of becoming big business.[9] The training and teaching that Lifeline offered was good - the harm reduction ethos at the heart of its objectives, providing a basic grounding in motivational interviewing, drug use paraphernalia and risks, and knowledge of the range of services available to its drug-using clients. The idea of the needle exchange was to give out new needles in exchange for used ones, which - if used again - increased the risk of HIV, hepatitis, and other blood borne infections. Through this interaction with drug users, who were largely reluctant to use mainstream health services because of the stigmatising effects of their criminalised usage, services were introduced and offered to potentially support people by engaging in various drug treatment programmes.

After I familiarised myself with the various sizes of needle, plus some basic health-promotion knowledge, I worked with experienced staff members one day a week on a voluntary basis. People who inject drugs come from all walks of life and in different shapes and sizes. The contrasting effects of the drugs soon became evident to me. I became adept at spotting who was there due to heroin use, amphetamine use, or steroid use. The latter (in the minority) tended to be pumped up, muscle bound and anxious to get in and out of the needle exchange as swiftly as possible. By contrast, most of the heroin users had emaciated frames, slow reaction times and multiple health problems. A trained nurse was on hand to attend to the various problems, including incredibly odorous gangrene. The last major group, amphetamine users - of which there were only a few - were predictably 'wired', often exhibiting collapsed jaws through endless chewing and gurning.

The vast majority who attended the needle exchange were grateful and polite, and no doubt appreciated being treated like fellow human beings. Although there wasn't enough time to get to know anyone properly, there was time to chat. I heard many sad stories - of life on the streets, periods in prison and of being brought up in care. Working there, I got to know the city's Big Issue sellers, and they would subsequently greet me and shout out in a friendly manner. Popularity at last!

As well as harm minimisation, through the exchange of needles, Lifeline also handed out free condoms. I must have lived a sheltered life before this as I didn't realise there were so many types, sizes, colours and flavours - some with ribbed textures, others specifically designed for anal use which was quite an eye-opener. They were largely collected by sex workers from the local area. My standard question, after greeting those who attended the project, was "Any returns?" - meaning, of course, needles. It became less automatic upon receiving the reply, "You wouldn't want my returns, love!"

My colleagues at the needle exchange were a friendly, down-to-earth bunch, some of whom had experienced drug or alcohol problems of their own. Others, like myself, were people who had taken drugs as part of the club culture at the time. No doubt some of the attraction of working there was its informal approach compared to statutory services. Staff here were encouraged to be open, discussing their own drug use with those that used the project, thus helping to break down barriers. This side of the job was something I enjoyed immensely and felt comfortable with.

After working at the needle exchange for six months, I applied and was successful in gaining a paid position within the project. This was as a casework development officer at a new service, not yet set up - ultimately, a structured day service in the Openshaw area of Manchester. The area was being regenerated after suffering decades of neglect. This was in conjunction with substantial investments in the eastern part of the city, through Manchester City Football Club, newly based there. The fresh project was largely funded by 'New Deal' regeneration monies, made available in the area. I met various staff based at the huge, local New Deal office and it was striking just how big an industry regeneration appeared to be.

The project was aimed at drug and alcohol users who needed structure in their days to compensate for the massive hole at the centre of their lives - formerly filled with the pursuit and consumption of substances.

After the invaluable experience gained at the needle exchange, I now witnessed one of the more problematic sides of the Lifeline project - perhaps symptomatic of issues within the voluntary sector as a whole. From the outset there was pressure in the form of targets; criteria applied to get people in and bums on seats. Despite our best efforts to set up a variety of activities - sports, arts, meditation - and promote the centre through community groups and services, the uptake for places was painfully slow. There was little training, and what in-house guidance we did get was largely irrelevant to our roles. We were thus left to fend for ourselves - making it up as we went along.

I do have some fond memories of the time, including a drumming workshop run by a hippie who had perhaps ingested too many substances himself. He was 'mad as a ship's cat' (professional diagnosis, obviously) and his sense of rhythm left a lot to be desired. There was also a meditation session where various participants fell asleep - one of whom was audibly farting throughout, altering the desired spiritual balance and atmosphere. Both occasions led to uncontrollable gales of laughter from participants and staff.

Such buoyant moments were few and far between, however, and my time there was tarnished by poor relationships with the project managers. Within eight months of starting the job, I was the last of the original staff - the rest having voted with their feet. This, I believe, was largely due to the actions of one manager - Myra - who was ego-driven, pretentious and at times, tyrannical.

Myra seemed to do very little work herself, but had a great penchant for 'dressing down' staff in front of others, highlighting their perceived flaws or tasks that remained unfinished. I remember her telling off an admin worker in front of staff and visitors for revealing to another agency - quite accurately - that our project was "quiet"; her retort - that such insight was a "confidential business matter". On another occasion, she criticised me for my "homophobic language" after I told a colleague that I was going outside for "a fag".

I also had the added grievance that Lifeline, or certainly the one manager therein, would not allow me time off for a placement which was part of my social work qualification. I therefore contemplated having to take a year off from my studies. As there was no guarantee this situation wouldn't arise the year after, I followed the example of my colleagues and resigned.[10]

During my work at Lifeline, I established contacts at countless local services and came to realise there was always work available (casual bank stuff) if I needed it. For the next year or so - while I completed my social work qualification - I worked for Turning Point, putting stints in at its Crisis Point project (a short-stay mental health project) and its Wellington Road project (a longer-term residential project for those with serious and enduring mental health issues). These experiences were good ones, and I regarded such projects as well run. There were many excellent and highly-experienced staff - some of whom are still friends to this day (even the staff member, unnamed for legal reasons, who regularly answered the internal phone to residents, "Hello, KFC - can I take your order?").

This work kept me going while I concluded my studies, and colleagues were supportive during a somewhat tumultuous time in my personal life. I found myself in an in-between partners situation - all of my own making, I must add (you really don't need to know the sordid details).

The week after I split from my girlfriend, I was involved in an accident, which added to my sense of personal chaos. I had taken a taxi to the Wellington Road project for a morning shift, still bleary-eyed from the night before - spent feeling sorry for myself in an inebriated state - when the car behind shunted into us. There was no great damage to the taxi and - as I arrived at work - I felt a bit of mild shock, that was all. However, as time went on, my neck stiffened and became painful when I moved - to the extent that my excellent manager, Carla, took me straight to A&E at Manchester Royal Infirmary. I was asked to wait in triage, lying flat on a bed with my neck immobilised in a cervical collar. In this completely helpless state, I spotted Helen, a resident from Wellington Road,[11] walking towards me having noticed my presence. Unbeknown to me at the time, she'd been admitted to hospital the day before after self-harming (cutting herself across the neck). She was a lovely, if extremely damaged woman, and normally I wouldn't have objected to talking to her. However, it certainly wasn't what I needed in my rather pathetic state, and I was glad to see a staff member guide her away from me.

After a full morning at the hospital, I was given the inevitable diagnosis of whiplash. The X-rays showed no major damage and I was given some strong painkillers, then discharged home. In a thoroughly dazed state, with a cup of tea and the television on, I observed a mouse running across the living room carpet, stopping to eyeball me. Completely unperturbed by my presence, it nonchalantly scampered off into the kitchen. So, as well as being 'chucked', left to lead a solitary existence, in pain and not knowing when I would work again, I now had an infestation of streetwise, cocky mice.

The moral of the story is that we all feel completely shat on at times, but such periods do pass. You have to believe that and keep your chin up, which, when suffering from whiplash, is also sound medical advice.

~ ~ ~

During this period, I received the news about the death of my brother, David. He was ten years older than me which partly explains why we were never close. His dependence on alcohol - evident since his youth - had spiralled out of control during his adult years. And although pneumonia had provided the final, fatal touch, it was definitely drinking that killed him. After many years without contact, it was a great surprise then just how well I got on with his friends. They all said how alike we were - in manner and sense of humour - leaving me with regrets over not getting to know him as an adult. I related far better to David's friends than I did the rest of my family. Grief doesn't necessarily bring people together, and relations with them at the funeral were as strained as ever.

~ ~ ~

The final part of my social work qualification was an 80-day placement designed to give work experience, hopefully in a service relevant to the student's career interests. Such placements could be sources of much consternation as many students were unhappy with where they were stationed. For me, fortunately, it was a perfect fit. I was placed with the N'Gage Assertive Outreach Team[12] in Manchester. The group, again in the voluntary sector, worked with those experiencing serious mental health problems, including psychotic symptoms and the tendency to disengage from mainstream services. Many had a dual diagnosis, essentially meaning that as well as complex mental health problems they also had drug and/or alcohol dependency issues, thus needed a more intensive approach.

One of the most significant cases during my student training was that of Mrs J, a well-known figure on the streets of Moss Side where she was identified as an active player in one of the gangs (notorious in the early 2000s for ongoing drug wars). She was an indomitable character - quick to anger, with a mouthful of invective and always ready to prove her toughness. Like many colourful characters though, she had outer layers which disguised her vulnerability (resulting from years of abuse). Her bark was usually worse than her bite.

Mrs J had a long-standing diagnosis of paranoid schizophrenia, as well as a long-term dependence on drugs, mainly crack cocaine. She funded this habit through sex work - selling herself on the streets, as well as turning tricks for gang members when directed. Dangers and the risk of assault are part and parcel of such work, but Mrs J had the force of personality not easily ascribed under the title 'victim'. She was adept at manipulating situations to her own ends, and staff at N'Gage had to be constantly on alert checking that she wasn't utilising their support for illicit means. I remember her calmly walking to our car from a doorway, en-route to an appointment at her solicitor's - hotly followed by a large man shouting abuse. What she had been doing was ambiguous and debatable, but she was nonetheless admonished by my colleague who understandably didn't want his services to include that of 'getaway car'.

She was, certainly at first, an intimidating figure to get to grips with - particularly for a trainee social worker. But, over time, we developed a good working relationship and she became my primary case for the purposes of this final placement.

Through this work, I became well acquainted with local solicitors and the Magistrates' Court on Minshull Street which was a regular haunt. Mrs J was subject to one of the first uses nationally of Anti-Social Behaviour legislation in the form of a Premises Closure Order. These new powers allowed Police to evict her from her home in Moss Side which, they alleged, had become a 'crack den'. There had been long-standing complaints from neighbours about gang members congregating there. Although the social work team had witnessed similar scenes, they contended that the reality wasn't as clear cut (certainly in the way it was depicted in the local media) and that she was as much victim as perpetrator. Either way, the legal framework for these orders was Civil (judged according to the 'balance of probability'), rather than Criminal where level of proof has to be 'beyond reasonable doubt'.

There were many weeks of preliminary hearings, cancellations and sentencing reports. At court, Mrs J seemed resigned to such bureaucracy and often used her time there to catch up and socialise. She seemed to know many of the people waiting to be processed, which included members of her extended family. The demographic of most of the defendants was evidence of a parallel universe populated by those on the bottom rung of society. They were people who were products of neglect and abuse, whose lives had been criminalised through drug use and blighted by mental health problems, together with the chaos that comes with that; overall, they lived a modern-day 'Dickensian' existence and Mrs J was very much at home among them.

Although she could never be described as innocent, Mrs J was still vulnerable. The term 'cuckooing' is now frequently used to describe this scenario whereby drug users/dealers take over the home of a vulnerable person in order to use it as a base. It is a crime that has become increasingly common, and I have encountered it in my work life on numerous occasions.

We helped Mrs J find new, temporary accommodation while the search for a long-term solution to her housing needs was examined. The last time I saw Mrs J was five years later, towards the end of a works night out. I spotted her standing in the shadows on the pavement as we headed into a restaurant on Rusholme's Curry Mile. She was obviously plying her trade and did a double take when I said hello; recognition finally setting in as she addressed me as "that bloody social worker". She was her usual self - friendly, but wary, yet managed to cadge a fag off me. At the end of a long night, my friends remarked how I always seemed to know the classiest of people. Mrs J was very much a 'survivor' and I hope that she's still around to this day.[13]

Another fascinating character I met while at N'Gage was George. I played a part in helping him to move in to a new flat on Victoria Square, Ancoats - the first municipal housing estate in Manchester. Built in 1894, the place is Grade II listed and surrounds a beautiful courtyard. (It is a shame that practically all social housing since has not lived up to the aesthetic standards of this estate.)

George's appearance had been ravaged by years of homelessness and an enduring psychotic illness. It was thus difficult to tell how old he was. He had retained his charm nonetheless courtesy of a beautiful, gentle, lilting Scottish accent, through which he addressed all the female members of staff as "m'dear". He was, alas, deeply embedded in his own world and remained an enigma. He often wore a kilt and an old jumper as he began his daily travels around the streets of Manchester. It was heart-warming to see him content in his new flat, even though he proceeded to decorate the walls with scientific diagrams and equations. (In his younger days, he had apparently been a radio controller in the British Army.) I was later thrilled to find out that his image had been immortalised in a painting exhibited at Manchester Art Gallery – one depicting him living on the streets.

My time at N'Gage taught me a lot, and I was impressed by the level of dedication and experience within the team. This was my last encounter working in the voluntary sector, and my involvement with it thereafter would be in the capacity of commissioning and reviewing roles.

I have seen projects that are well run with good staff and some that are less impressive. The same, however, could be said of those still operated in the public sector. I've seen providers - certainly through my mixed experiences inside the Lifeline project - that have become victims of their own success, and subsequently overreached themselves, leading to their ultimate demise. I've also witnessed distrust and general dislike between providers - the result, perhaps, of competition in the care market, but also evidence of 'sectarian mindsets' (which I observed earlier on the fringes of the political left).

Part of the problem is the bidding and contracting arrangements by which much of the voluntary sector is governed. Contracts of provision are short term - often around three years in length - and this can lead to a rapid turnover of providers, resulting in destabilisation and inconsistency, more so for those using the service. It also contributes to the regular loss of experienced staff; emphasis put on chasing contracts, rather than the core work of the provider and thus the happiness of existing staff.

Other aspects, such as lack of trade union recognition and involvement, still concern me. And I am personally more comfortable with the sector being split into small, innovative entities which can then be at the forefront of providing services where there are gaps in provision. This contrasts with taking over former public sector services as part of a privatisation agenda. I say this not as a criticism of the many dedicated people who work in the sector (and who knows, I might be joining them at some point in the future), but because of the destructive nature of the cuts in public sector provision over the last decade. Their work is now more vital than ever; the rise in food banks one stark example of this.

~ ~ ~

I'd made a mess of my personal life and had no bedrock of family support to fall back on. There were the inevitable, divided loyalties and parting of the waves that follow relationship breakups, and I felt more alone than at any other time in my adult life. The shoddy way I'd treated women in my life left me with overbearing feelings of guilt and I convinced myself that I deserved to be lonely. During this period of self-recrimination, I drank too much and felt bloody sorry for myself. And rumination, as is always the case, produced no earth-shattering revelations or answers to my self-made problems.

I had to somehow find a way forward. Because backward was a mess.

Despite the state of disarray in my life, I managed to complete my studies. And my experience in the voluntary sector gave me the practical knowledge needed for the next chapter of my life…as a qualified social worker.

Chapter 7 - Mrs B

Proper northern, in all its best senses, Mrs B was big, loud and abrasive, with a colourful gob of insults for anyone that crossed her. She had a fearsome reputation at the Oldham Community Mental Health Team, and eyebrows were raised when her case was reallocated to the new, inexperienced social worker. Me.[14]

In 2004, I was in my late thirties, and this was my first, post-qualifying job after recently completing a degree in Social Work at Salford University. I was also new to the town of Oldham. My only experience of the place was attending an outdoor music festival at Werneth Park in the mid-90s, plus a late night football match at Boundary Park against my team, Carlisle United. The result was 3-1 to the Latics, but I have little recollection of the game (burying traumatic memories is a coping strategy which allows the mind to function without ruminating on past distress) apart from it being the coldest experience of my life. Unbeknown to me, Oldham's ground was well known for its arctic temperatures.

What little else I knew about the place didn't exactly show it in a positive light. At a Man City versus Oldham game, I heard Blues' fans regale their Oldham counterparts with the chant *"BIFFO!"* This somewhat derogatory moniker, as is the way with football fans, was an acronym for *'Big Ignorant Fucker From Oldham'*. The letters were used flexibly depending on the object of the insult, and could be changed to *'Idle Fucker'* or *'Ignorant Fat Fucker'* if need be. I'm sure you get the gist.

The reputation of Oldham was scarred by riots in 2001 when pitched battles ensued between white and Asian youths. As part of my job, I inevitably had to wander around districts of Oldham labelled 'no-go areas' due to the bitter divisions that existed (often lost, but then saved by my trusty A-Z map).[15] Whatever the standing of the town though, or the debatable kernels of truth that lay within it, this was to be the place where I would find love, stability and many good friends. And is the place where I have lived and worked ever since.

Despite the varied work experience behind me, my new team was partially right in thinking that nothing could prepare me for working with Mrs B. Some found it hard to believe that I didn't know her, or at least know *of her*. After all, *everyone* knew Mrs B! My explanation of being new to the town didn't cut it.

I prepared myself by reading her file - paperwork handwritten and mostly illegible - and acquainted myself with her history and risk profile. It was therefore with some trepidation that I visited Mrs B for the first time at her flat, near the centre of Oldham. My initial impression was of a larger-than-life character, displaying warmth and aggression in equal measure - and at equal volume. Loud. Very Loud! I wouldn't say that she was unwelcoming, but she *did* have a litany of complaints about the team ("They don't bloody listen to me") and some exacting requirements with regard to my role ("The least you can do is answer the phone when I ring").

I could imagine what her impression was of me - the bald, skinny, softly spoken social worker at her door. (It may be of interest to some that my looks at this time had been compared to that of the self-promoting, dance music vegan, Moby. Now, when I look in the mirror, I see the withered reflection of Walter White from Breaking Bad. That's a lifetime of social work for you. Don't do it, kids!) To get a word in edgeways took maximum assertiveness on my part. I suspected the cat on her lap was probably hard of hearing as it lay there unflinching and undisturbed throughout this first meeting.

Mrs B reminded me of the northern, working-class woman played by Les Dawson in the 'Cissie and Ada' sketches. Between loud utterances there was a similar miming of words and phrases, replete with the exasperated grabbing of her boob for comic effect. The original purveyors of this art form were Lancashire millworkers who devised a way to communicate amidst the clanking sound of machinery. It was with relief, therefore, that I observed this humorous side beneath her bluster and also vulnerable and sensitive shades to her character.

Now in her late fifties, Mrs B had spent much of her life in and out of mental health wards - partly as an informal patient, and partly under Section 3 of the 1983 Mental Health Act.[16] She was one of many in Oldham who still referred to the wards at the Royal Oldham Hospital as "The Bottom Block". The hospital, built on the site of a former workhouse, had its own male and female 'Imbecile' blocks. After the advent of the National Health Service in 1948, the former workhouse infirmary became known as Boundary Park General Hospital, which included an annex specialising in psychiatric and geriatric care – aka the bottom block. By the time I worked in Oldham, the mental health wards had been at Parklands House - within the hospital - for many years, but plenty of people still used the old, rather grim title. I daresay the defensive refrain of "You're not putting *me* in the bottom block" is still heard.

Throughout her troubled life, Mrs B had various diagnoses assigned to her by the consultant psychiatrists. Most pointed to a form of mood disorder with bi-polar traits, whilst others emphasised behavioural issues under the general title of personality disorder; highlighting poor coping skills and emotional instability. Few of these dry assessments shed much light on the complexity and reality of her difficulties though, borne as they were from a lifetime of abuse and exploitation, alongside a corresponding shortage of being valued and loved.

Some of Mrs B's problems did, admittedly, stem from poor decision making - especially in her choice of friends and sexual partners. Beneath her loud abrasiveness some saw the side of her that was easy-going and therefore a vulnerable target. Her mood was disrupted by this – people who exploited her generous nature; stealing money, food and cigarettes. She was a regular caller at the office and on one occasion was in tears, bitterly complaining, "He's nicked me ciggies", asking that I replace the said items. When I refused, citing more pressing workload priorities, she became incensed. During another visit, she described - in lurid detail - her attraction to her current partner. "He's fookin massive, Richard!" When I said that I didn't need to know such intimate details in relation to her sex life, girth or otherwise, she collapsed into rasping, breathless laughter.

~ ~ ~

It's Monday morning, February 5th, 2005 - the sort of Monday which gives the day a bad name; a classic, northern scenario…pissing it down. The 'seen better days' windows in the office can barely resist the hammering from outside. I arrive back after an early visit to one of my service users, who's on a ward at Tameside Hospital. I'm met by Terry, my manager, who informs me that Mrs B has been on the phone asking for me. He says that she's in a "bit of a state", "in tears" and talking about "ending it all". He asks me to call her as soon as I can and seek him out for advice if I need to.

I phone her immediately and encounter Mrs B at her lowest, most despairing worst, wailing between breathless sobs saying she's "had enough" and "can't do it any more". I ask what's brought this on, but her response is garbled and confused. I manage to get a semblance of an answer though. It appears that her boyfriend has "took off" with some of her money. This pales into insignificance when she tells me that she has the pills ready and intends to take the lot of them. I persuade her to hold on until I get there.

I go straight to Terry's office and am relieved to find he's still there. Upon hearing my concern about her situation, he dampens my anxiety by offering to accompany me. It's still sheeting down with rain, but my relief is complete when he says we can go in his car.

Mrs B opens the door looking dishevelled. She is still in her dressing gown. We all sit down. Terry offers to make a brew while she talks to me, but she refuses, crouches in her chair and sobs. After the tears subside, she manages to mutter a few words. "I've had it…he's gone, all me money, me DLA[17]…I only got it yesterday!"

Terry knows her well and is unobtrusive while he sits listening, but still manages to become the object of her erupting anger. "And what the hell are you fookin' lookin' at?"

Another period of silence ensues and I'm unsure of how or whether to break it. The tears, anger and self-recrimination take over. She is inconsolable.

Terry asserts himself which makes me feel a bit out of my depth - inadequate even. He calmly goes through the options with her, not mentioning the packets of medication on the table. We can refer her to the Mental Health Crisis Team who will visit her at home to check on her welfare or request a bed on a mental health ward.

Mrs B is well versed with the limited coin flip and immediately opts for the hospital bed. She turns to me and wails, "I can't do it. I can't keep safe." Then she grabs me for a hug, adding to the dampness of my coat with her tears and snot.

I wrench my neck and spine back into place. She is a big woman in every sense and has a wrestler's grip. I am the Syd Little to her Eddie Large. Before leaving to make arrangements, I ask about her cat.

"She's been living next door. Even she's fookin' deserted me!"

The anguish is real, without a hint of irony or a smile.

~ ~ ~

As I was still new to the job, Terry took me through the process of requesting a bed for an informal, voluntary admission, accessed through a 'gatekeeper' after consultation with a psychiatrist. Hospital beds on mental health wards are severely rationed, and so I had to explain the reasons, risks and urgency of the situation. The process always starts with the aim of sourcing a bed as near as possible to the patient's home. Over the years this became increasingly difficult though, with people being transported as far away as Wrexham and Liverpool - symptomatic of the ever-increasing bed shortages in the NHS. On this occasion we were in luck. A bed was accessed for Mrs B at Parklands House, Royal Oldham Hospital.

Terry was fantastic in how he supported me that day and remains a good friend now that he's retired. In Mrs B's case the risks were real. She had tried and come close to killing herself in the past. Comprehensively assessing such risks is near-impossible of course and one of the hardest, most anxiety-provoking tasks undertaken when working in mental health. I started to develop a 'sixth sense' over when to act after hearing people tell me about their suicidal thoughts. That and when to just listen. It wasn't merely about asking the right questions, but getting a feel for the person - knowing how they react to stressors in life. We're all capable of getting it wrong though. I don't know anyone in the field who hasn't had sleepless nights thinking about worst-case scenarios when dealing with such fragile souls. Guidance from experienced team members like Terry was invaluable therefore, particularly as I was a novice.

~ ~ ~

Despite the best efforts of those who work on mental health wards, they can be scary places for both patients and staff alike. Volatile outbursts, shouting and screaming are commonplace - punctuated as they are by acutely unwell people. Despite this, they can also be asylums in the best sense of the word - providing refuge for those in crisis, such as Mrs B.

I visited Mrs B on the ward during her first week there. She had improved, but her mood was still volatile, changing like the flick of a switch from depressive tears to vicious, angry outbursts (as I found out during her ward round[18]). As far as I could make out, the discussion was going perfectly well, without any great bones of contention. As an informal patient, Mrs B was free to leave the ward as she pleased, but was advised - at this early stage - that if she wished to take such a path then she should seek support from ward staff or the Community Mental Health Team (CMHT). During a break in the meeting, she told me, unequivocally, that she disagreed with this benign consensus.

"And what the fuck's the point of you, if you're just going to sit there nodding?"

The fact that I *did* agree, and she did too in essence, was of no consequence. I sensed that she thought I should be loudly advocating on her behalf, arguing the toss and thumping the table, issuing demands like a 1970s caricature of a trade union official. "The aspirations of my members and I are not being met with such an offer. Everybody out!" I tried to express, in the understated way that was more my style, that I felt the advice given was constructive and in her best interest. These 'flimsy' sentiments did not meet with her approval though, and she stubbornly refused to speak to me for the next two weeks - telling ward staff and doubtless everyone within earshot that I was "fookin' useless".

Once again, I was glad of the reassurance from my team, who - whilst laughing - told me that Mrs B had done exactly the same to them, and that she would "soon come round".

I was reminded of some of the theory I learned on the social work course which emphasised that although the aim is to establish a 'therapeutic relationship' with service users, this is different to a friendship or advocacy. Sometimes as a social worker we have to act in the person's 'best interest', even if this goes against their express wishes. An example of this is when I had to section someone for treatment because they were too mentally unwell to make a rational decision. Relationships formed thus always have the potential for conflict and I learnt to develop a 'thick skin'.

As predicted, Mrs B and I got back on track and developed a good working relationship after her discharge from hospital. She spent three weeks on the ward, during which her anti-depressant medication was altered, and she managed to recuperate a little both mentally and physically. Her confidence and self-esteem were still low though, and so - acting on advice from my line manager, Anne, during supervision - I referred her to a support worker within the CMHT.[19] The introduction of Dianne helped reduce my workload as the day-to-day tasks (benefit applications, contact with the GP etc.) and regular phone calls were now shared. The extra support also helped Mrs B engage in more activities as a distraction from her ongoing problems. Plus, she could 'sound off' to someone else.

Although I reduced my contact with Mrs B in terms of planned visits and phone calls, I still saw her regularly around Oldham town centre or when I travelled on the bus. I didn't drive, which meant that I saw service users on an informal basis more often than my colleagues. This had its pros *and* cons, but Mrs B was usually friendly when I saw her. In fact, I often *heard* her before seeing her and became accustomed to the cry, "Hiya, love!" from afar.

On one occasion, she saw me getting on the '83' bus and announced to everyone on the bottom deck, "This is me social worker. He came with me for my breast screening last week."

After she clocked the quizzical expressions on the passengers' faces, she at least saved me a little. "No, he didn't come *in* with me!" - catching her breath between bouts of distinctive, rasping laughter. I have been 'outed' as a social worker in a similar fashion many times since. The passengers' reactions that day contrasted with the usual mixture of mothers shielding their children, minor levels of hostility and downright indifference.

The biggest factor improving Mrs B's stability at this time was no doubt her reintroduction to the Phoenix Day Centre. Funded by Oldham Council, the facility was a specialist service for those struggling with mental health problems. There were various activities available, including those run by people who used the mental health services themselves (self-organised, self-help groups as they were known in the trade). They included therapeutic groups to help people manage anxiety, groups to cope with hearing voices, plus many other educational and recreational pursuits. The place, however imperfect, was a lifeline for those who would otherwise be socially isolated; the wider community often unable to understand their behaviour and deep-seated problems.[20]

Mrs B had attended the centre for many years, before her hospital episode. She'd stopped going after one too many blazing arguments with the management committee though. Dianne and I used our finest diplomatic skills (pleading, grovelling, and then pleading again) which fortunately allowed her to attend again - initially on a trial basis. Although another argument was habitually just around the corner (she loved a good barney, after all), she managed to curtail her excesses before too much damage was done.

I finished working with Mrs B just before the closure of the Phoenix centre. In cold, social work parlance, her case was closed too. She was still supported by staff at the CMHT, but I wasn't directly involved with this. I still, however, saw her around town and such coincidences were always a delight.

In her twilight years she became increasingly unsteady on her feet - eventually using a Motability scooter to get out and about. When I say 'using', what I really mean is driving at top speed, causing unsuspecting pedestrians to be flung out of the way or risk serious injury. Her skills at the wheel were haphazard at best - the ingenuity of a one-handed maniac, reluctant to let go of her ever-present fag. Whether her reckless driving resulted in fatalities is unknown.

My last recollection of Mrs B is of her on said scooter alongside another elderly lady, sat in her own deadly contraption. They drove at the same high speed, giving the people in front of them the fright of their lives. This was not, it seemed, a couple of old, physically frail, disabled women, but rather a Panzer division.

Mrs B died in 2012. It was long after any official involvement from me and so I wasn't party to any information concerning the cause of death. I have little doubt that years of extreme emotions, plus despair, anxiety and chain smoking will have contributed to her downfall.

I remember her with great fondness though.

Chapter 8 - Secure Hospitals

Throughout my time as a social worker, I spent many days visiting people in secure units. As part of a multi-disciplinary team, my role was to establish therapeutic relationships with these people; not easily achievable when faced with complex needs and locked wards hardly conducive to rapport and trust. The wards were often noisy and intimidating places, with the more extreme regimes echoing the feeling of prison – in contrast to the therapeutic places of safety they were supposed to be. Secure units are often many miles from home, meaning that families have to travel great distances and pay exorbitant parking fees for the privilege of visiting their loved ones.

In the UK, secure hospitals house those with severe and enduring mental health problems, who need long term care and supervision because of the risks they pose to themselves and/or others. They are generally referred from acute, short stay mental health wards, once their mental health issues are deemed too risky and complex to be dealt with in the community; or indeed inside prisons when a psychiatrist decides that the chief determinant of a crime (the *index* offence) is the individual's mental illness.

Levels of monitoring and supervision in secure hospitals are largely in harmony with the degree of risk - defined as low, medium or high. As a rough guide, the majority of people situated in both high and medium secure units come through the forensic route, whilst low secure units tend to house those with complex, treatment-resistant mental health issues, plus those from the former groups assessed as 'recovering' and therefore lower risk.[21]

The atmosphere of the units is generally defined by the security level. At one extreme, units feel like prisons. At the other, more like wards. All secure units require visitors to enter through an air-locked door, with ID, accompanied by ward staff. Possessions such as money, mobile phones, cigarettes and lighters - anything that can be potentially traded, or used as a weapon - are left in lockers at the entrance. Being led through the security apparatus often feels intimidating, and it is difficult initially not to feel defensive and on edge. The prison-like design adds to this unease. Many units have central viewing stations, secured with unbreakable glass; corridors around them in the style of a rotunda, allowing observation of all social interactions.[22] As well as severely limiting the privacy of the 'inmate', this also results in staff and visitors being permanently visible, with the unnerving sensation that all eyes are on you as you enter the building.

The design of the high secure units' interiors is deliberately low in stimulation, as these mostly accommodate those who are symptomatic in terms of delusional stimuli. In these units, privileges such as increased access to television, 'luxury' items and supervised leave are granted as rewards for good behaviour, increased engagement and co-operation. Although this is a clearly defined form of behavioural management, its opposite effect is that of reinforcing bitterness and hopelessness after incidents of bad behaviour (when basic privileges are withdrawn).

I still remember my first visit to one ward on the site of the old Prestwich Hospital in Manchester.[23] The occupants' favourite activity seemed to be body building (staff included) and everyone there appeared to be six feet tall and four foot wide - mental health's very own American football team, in contrast to me, the pallid, skinny but interesting sort.

Another memorable visit was during a placement, as part of my social work training. I entered a ward at Tameside Hospital and was greeted with the sight of patients watching Big Brother live (in the early 2000s when people still did stuff like this). I had an attack of 'irony overdose' (Alanis Morissette, take note) gazing at incarcerated people taking satisfaction from *other* incarcerated people while seemingly ignoring their own oppressive environment.

In some of the harsher regimes, male-only wards can act like testosterone-driven environments. This survival of the fittest masculine hierarchy often inhibits honest communication though and is a barrier to progress. It *is* possible to reach beyond such a stalemate when seeing 'inmates' on a one-to-one basis - getting underneath masculine surfaces and witnessing vulnerable, flawed and frightened specimens beneath - however, this isn't always doable, and developing trusting relationships which prompt people to let their guard down is difficult when only visiting on an occasional basis.[24]

Many of the units, just like prisons, experience problems with street drugs being smuggled. This has been especially evident over the last ten years with the wide distribution of Spice - a synthetic, laboratory-made drug. Instances of psychotic episodes linked to the use of this drug - plus bartering within the wards - add to an 'us and them' secretive culture.

An enduring myth, heard through many sources, and certainly a favourite of the tabloids, is that hospital is a soft option preferred by those playing the mental health card. In reality, the average time spent in hospital custody is *longer* than in prison (for comparable offences), so such a strategy doesn't make sense. In the most notorious of cases - Ian Brady, the Moors murderer, for example - patients are detained in hospital for life. There is no right to parole and discharge can only take place after being authorised by the Ministry of Justice, which can take an incredibly long time. And this is only *after* the multi-disciplinary team, consultant psychiatrist and mental health tribunal judge have decided that the person is fit for discharge. Add to this the inevitable wait - once the MoJ have rubber stamped things - for the social worker to perform his/her magic, source and successfully apply for funding for appropriate supported accommodation in the community, and the idea of hospital being a soft option starts to come apart.

I would suggest that all those social media keyboard warrior 'judges' who assert that holiday camp conditions exist in such places perhaps try them out for themselves. I'm sure with the contacts I still have, that this can be arranged.

~ ~ ~

The grim picture that I've painted of bodybuilder staff and the like is not representative of the *entire* secure hospitals structure. Even in the most austere units, there are dedicated and skilled staff who seek to provide humane responses to the complex issues they face. And at the other end of the spectrum, there are pioneering units which act like rehabilitation centres. Inside these, activities are encouraged in order to improve the abilities and skill set of the patient in preparation for an independent life outside. Therapeutic approaches designed to improve cognitive (coping) skills and practical, functional capability involve psychological, therapy-based methods such as relapse prevention, drugs and alcohol awareness, and activities such as cookery and educational courses - all aimed at increasing independence. Such traits are often sadly lacking - some patients having no experience of taking responsibility for even basic, household duties, and others suffering the negative symptoms of psychotic illness, leaving them demotivated and de-skilled. Many more are institutionalized after years in a ward environment where meals and cleaners are provided; decisions about daily life thus taken by others.[25]

I have seen patients struggle to make the most basic of decisions. In a local shop, one asked for guidance about whether to buy a bottle of diet coke or 'full fat'. Others displayed classic, post-prison behaviour such as waiting for me to open doors before walking through.

My contact with patients mainly revolved around attendance at CPA (Care Programme Approach) review meetings and mental health tribunals. CMHT practitioners were also required to compile Social Circumstances Reports for tribunals. These aimed to provide a holistic picture of the person, rather than a narrowly-defined clinical report, including details about personal and family history, as well as their wishes and aspirations. The role of a CMHT staff member, nurse or social worker is most acute when discharge from a hospital is imminent. At this point participating in review meetings and tribunals is vital, whereas the rest of the time it is the ward clinical team who play the greater role.

Mental health tribunals are empowered by law to adjudicate over a patient's detention in relation to their treatment and mental health condition. They are run through independent review hearings where professionals are asked to justify detainment and discuss future planning and care in the context of eventual discharge.[26]

The formal, quasi-legalistic atmosphere of a tribunal hearing *can* be intimidating, and is often too much for some patients. In addition, the uncomfortable experience of listening while people talk at length about you and your behaviour discourages many from attending. Some are too ill to attend, or have different priorities on the day. Others, however - particularly those with grandiose ideas - relish the chance to address the forum, even when their solicitor, or advocate, advise against it.

Mr C was one such patient who wished to take on hearings with great gusto. On one occasion he interrupted a consultant psychiatrist who was describing a violent altercation between Mr C and another 'inmate'. Mr C, speaking with great, assumed authority, interjected: "I think that Dr Mustapha will find, if he refers to his records, that I wasn't even present on the ward that day. I remember this specifically being the day that Roger Moore invited me for lunch, after skiing in the Swiss Alps. Look it up. It was on his birthday! Therefore, I ask the panel to disregard this evidence. You can ask Roger if you like."

Mr C's delusional framework involved many famous figures. And he constantly rejected the option of being discharged from hospital - to a supported, housing facility - claiming that he had a "perfectly good" house in Oldham, that had been left for him in "the Queen Mother's will". The plausibility of his already feeble argument was not helped when he referred to one of the nurses there as "Idi Amin's brother".

Another man famous for his dramatic tribunal appearances was Mr D. He had a perfectly valid complaint regarding Clozaril, the side effect of which was weight gain and increased chest dimensions; larger "man boobs", as he called them. Despite being advised not to reveal this 'sumptuous' sight – i.e. his favourite party trick - he proceeded to treat those present to a glimpse of his magnificent, pendulous 'breasts'. Most greeted this image with a resigned expression, given that he was well known for such stripping prowess. Others on the panel, new to this rumbustious show, were left traumatised.

Among those with fixed, delusional ideas, disinhibited behaviour was common. There would be occasions when they initially came across to the panel as reasonable and rational, but after one too many searching questions such a cover was torpedoed by their bizarre beliefs.[27] One man, disarmingly affable, despite his conviction that all staff were conspiring with a secret cult to keep him imprisoned, often ended up dismissing panel members as fellow plotters; individuals engaged in planting messages in his brain.

Tribunal hearings can be a nervy affair for professional staff - especially the uninitiated. I was known at my place of work for always dressing up for such occasions - in contrast to my normal, laid-back appearance. I wore a shirt and tie, and my suit pants became known as my 'tribunal trousers'. They helped me mentally prepare for the potential grilling ahead. The one time I'd worn my jeans, I felt inferior to the formally-attired panel, which made it easier for them to look down on me and my profession.

The potential for confrontation increases when the subject of a hearing is close to being discharged from hospital. At this point pressure mounts on the community team to find alternative accommodation for the person about to move on. There is a huge imbalance between supply and demand in the supported housing market. Most of the supply comes from the voluntary sector, but with an increasing share from the private sector. Because available facilities are subject to huge demand though, there are often long, prohibitive waiting lists which need tackling when trying to secure a place for a patient. It is a very common scenario for a patient who has been assessed, and is ready for discharge, to spend time waiting for appropriate accommodation; like being indefinitely ghosted by a removal firm.

As the social worker explaining this situation to a tribunal hearing, it was often uncomfortable, and I felt that I was being blamed for a lack of facilities. Solicitors are highly trained and skilled and made a habit of cutting through deliberate vagueness on my part. When providing answers regarding availability, the solicitor would try to tease a timeframe out of me, despite this being out of my control.

At one hearing, the chair of the panel - an overfed judge - was a major thorn in my side; such an experience bringing home the reality and class hierarchy at play within the judiciary. This 'man', who I unfortunately met on two occasions, had an unworldly disdain for those lower than him on the social ladder. In conversations with colleagues, I christened him the 'golf club brigadier' - usually found at the 19th hole, sozzled in a leather armchair. When it came to my turn in the spotlight, he introduced me by saying, "Now, we have Mr Wills. Your job title is that of social worker, is it not?"

I confirmed this was the case, noting the growling contempt with which he enunciated the title of my profession.

"And what is the purpose of your role at this hearing, Mr Wills?"

I explained that I had been liaising with accommodation providers in an attempt to source suitable housing for the patient to move into.

"I have read your report, Mr Wills. And it seems that you have so far been singularly unsuccessful in this role…"

He pronounced "unsuccessful" with such bemusement, that it could only be interpreted as questioning my competence. It was impossible therefore not to be a little defensive in my reply, as I explained that one service provider had accepted the referral but there was an inevitable waiting list for such procurements. There was a locking of horns between the judge and I regarding potential timescales - me being deliberately equivocal, and him equally *unequivocal* whilst dismissing the credibility of my answers. It was quite clear that I was on a hiding to nothing, but it didn't end there. As I left the hospital after the hearing, feeling rather deflated, I noticed the tribunal judge walking towards me. Our eyes met and he grimaced - emitting a sound which I can only describe as "Behrrr!"; a disdainful grunt similar in delivery to that of General Melchett, the character played by Stephen Fry in Blackadder.

Compounding such aristocratic ignorance was a general lack of understanding when it came to the availability of mental health resources. Taking Oldham as an example, things looked very different not so long ago. The 1991 Mental Illness Specific Grant meant funding to local authorities was ring-fenced in relation to mental health provision in the community e.g. supported housing and resettlement schemes. When I first started working for Oldham Council in 2004 there were many forms of supported housing available through the local authority - all of which have now gone. The termination of funding for patients moving from institutional to community care (plus austerity cuts in central government funding to local authorities) has undoubtedly contributed to this malaise.

While the general shortage of supported accommodation is a

definite problem, the design of the sector's provision is too, in that it hampers transitions from hospital. Services are based on the 'recovery model' which emphasises the need to help patients set goals and become increasingly independent. Accommodation is therefore short term - mostly set at two years. This is the right approach for many tenants / patients, but there is a significant minority in secure hospitals that do not suit this remit. Some have chronic and treatment-resistant mental health issues and need long-term support in order to function (independence a somewhat naïve aim). Unfortunately, despite years in rehabilitation wards, personal development ultimately plateaus. But there is very often nowhere else to go that will cater for their needs and keep them stable.

Many of those living in secure hospitals have incredibly complex problems, together with extreme forms of behaviour, which I intentionally don't give detailed accounts of because such patients wouldn't have the capacity to consent to. It would be unfair of me to elaborate therefore, except to say that caring for such individuals requires great patience, dedication and a level of professionalism unmatched elsewhere.

The social care sector has changed over the last twenty years with increasing reliance on private means. My last role within the Care Management and Review Team at Oldham Council was in a commissioning capacity - bidding for funding for services employed.[28] This meant becoming familiar with the eye-watering fees paid for such provision (known in the trade as 'shitloads'). Costs were well above a typical bed on a public sector ward, yet services were commissioned for the defective reason that no other provision was available. It doesn't take a soothsayer to realise that without increased investment in public sector provision, more of the NHS budget will be spent subsidising profits in the private sector. And all this *without* any noticeable improvement in the quality of service.

Secure mental health hospitals are a part of life that most do not see. Media depictions of them are often wide of the mark or dated. And however great *One Flew Over the Cuckoo's Nest* undoubtedly is, it doesn't capture the inner workings of a modern ward, or the intricate ramifications of political decisions on people. The reality is far more mundane: daily grind and long-term patient care for deeply damaged and complex individuals. But because such services are largely 'out of sight and out of mind' their resourcing will never be a priority in most voters' minds.

Chapter 9 - Mr S

Preparation for this chapter meant Mr S talking to me about his past and family background. And if it weren't for the limitations placed on us by Coronavirus, I would've liked to have been more collaborative in my approach. As it is, we spoke via the phone on numerous occasions and once the restrictions were lifted I visited him at home. He has reviewed what I have written and added vital details which illuminate his story. I have chosen not to include some of the more disturbing details of the abuse that he suffered and survived as he is not defined by this. I did not, therefore, want this chapter to be dominated and/or overshadowed by it.

~ ~ ~

I worked with Mr S for nearly 10 years. At the start of this period, I met Natalie - a CMHT support worker - on a work night out on Canal Street, Manchester. Completely smitten, I married her soon after my 40th birthday. After many rocky relationships in my 20s and 30s, I had finally found someone I wanted to be with for the rest of my life. She had two children, Jasmine and Sam, both young at the time, now independent and grown up. This was the family that helped me find stability and happiness – things which I had failed to bring about until then. Don't get me wrong, I *was* and *still am* a 'dour northern bastard', coming as I do from a long line of this proud, cultural form. Natalie & co, however, have provided constant support since - through the many pitfalls and tribulations that we call life.

~ ~ ~

Mr S is a warm, affable man in his mid-50s who lives a relatively quiet, but contented life in Shaw, a suburb of Oldham. He shares his home with a mate, and with his cat, Larry, who he is devoted to. His love of animals is one of his chief passions in life, alongside music (he used to be a well-known DJ in the area), clothes, charity shops and markets.

The facts of his - on the face of it - unremarkable existence only become revelatory when viewed in the context of his earlier experiences in life. Mr S spent most of his childhood, between the ages of four and sixteen, in care homes in the Cheshire area. He was a 'ward of the state', placed into care at this young age after his mother was admitted to hospital (in Stockport) and diagnosed with schizophrenia. Staff at the home said that his mother would eventually visit, but this never happened.

He did see his father and attempts were made for him to permanently return to the family home. But Mr S described his father as an alcoholic - a cruel and brutal man. He would whip him with his thick, leather belt and lock him in a room - sometimes a wardrobe - for hours on end. Mr S was finally kept at the children's home when his social worker realised how unhappy he was.

Later, on his 40th birthday, Mr S heard the news regarding his father's death. He had hanged himself.

Unfortunately, his experience of abuse didn't go away, but was compounded in various children's homes; mental, physical and sexual abuse at the hands of staff and their associates never far away. This story sadly echoes the experience of survivors of child sexual abuse from around the same time; powerless, vulnerable children targeted by predatory paedophile rings, involving the likes of Cyril Smith and Jimmy Savile.

Eight years old and having developed a love of animals, Mr S used to help out at a kennel near the home. Inexplicably, staff at the home permitted him to stay overnight, on weekends, at the kennel owner's house. The man made him sit on his knee and would then touch Mr S between his legs, before prompting him to reciprocate. Laying out girls' clothes on the bed, he also asked Mr S to dress up for him.

There were many more instances of abuse to both himself and others. Mr S has similar memories of episodes at a swimming pool - a leisure activity that he has avoided ever since. He endured sexual and physical abuse for over a decade. That was his life. These were his norms. Like many survivors, he buried these memories and only really made sense of them much later in life. At the time, he tried to resist such thoughts in the only way he knew - by being 'naughty' or 'acting up' which resulted in him being targeted for further abuse. He tells it now by saying he feels "lucky", as some children "had it far worse", and none of the sexual abuse that he experienced involved actual penetration.

After leaving care at the age of sixteen, Mr S joined the Army. This did not work out well. Following the onset of psychotic symptoms, he was medically discharged two years later, diagnosed with schizophrenia. The diagnosis of schizophrenia is often a contested one. Critics have highlighted a wide variety of symptoms or behaviour subsumed under this umbrella diagnosis which makes the term almost meaningless. A simple description of this most controversial of conditions is that it involves seeing, hearing, or believing things that, objectively, are not real. One thing that it is not, however, is the commonly misconceived 'twin personality'.[29] It is a bugbear of mine that many supposedly learned media commentators and intellectuals continue to misappropriate the term with such inaccuracy.

Mr S's symptoms have included visual hallucinations, such as faces watching him, audio hallucinations (repeated banging on the walls and ceiling) and the belief that certain people in his life command and control his behaviour. He is one of many that exhibit a clear link between childhood sexual abuse and psychotic symptoms in adulthood. Psychologists attribute this phenomenon to dissociation i.e. when a person disconnects their thoughts and emotions from what they experience. It is a common coping mechanism and is said to have a damaging effect on emotional development, which of course can lead to problems in adulthood.

Another clear pattern, which anyone working in mental health, homelessness, or alcohol/drug services will have observed, is that many service users come from a care background, or time in the armed forces. They report institutionalizing effects and emotional damage from their experiences, and admit to self-medicating with alcohol or drugs as a way of coping. I heard about such unspeakable, historic trauma and abuse in the lives of those that used our services to the point that I wasn't surprised if they presented in a challenging manner. I learnt not to expect those damaged by such experiences (which we can only envisage in our worst nightmares) to be pleasant, balanced or stable. Instead, I simply stood back from the surface bluster and bravado, and observed the vulnerable - often frightened - individual that lay within.

When I started working with Mr S, the damage of repeated trauma and abuse was clear. Having been admitted to hospital an estimated 22 times, he was well known to mental health services. And some of these were lengthy stays - often six months at a time. During these hospitalisations, he overdosed many times, and on one occasion tried to hang himself. Acts of violence towards others, including assaults on nursing staff, were also mentioned in reports. Despite this, CMHT and ward staff spoke of Mr S with great fondness - alongside the warning that he could be a 'handful' to work with.

Mr S's mental health problems were compounded by drug use, especially his long-term dependence on amphetamines; a habit acquired during the dance scene in the late 1980s when he was a DJ. Stimulants were rife at raves and often sustained users throughout the night. The big negative was a vicious comedown - physically and mentally. Symptoms included head and muscle aches, lethargy and fatigue, and low mood to the point of depression, tearfulness and irritability. I'd dabbled with speed in my twenties, but soon found out that the upside was not worth the downside; after-effects worse the older I became.

Mr S used speed on a regular basis and *not just* when he was partying. Unsurprisingly, as well as the comedowns, stimulants negatively impacted his psychotic symptoms, decreasing the efficacy of his medication. I also suspected that Mr S was financially exploited by local dealers, but there was insufficient evidence to back this up and he didn't trust me enough at this stage to disclose such information.

Predictably, his mood was erratic when I first started seeing him. At times, he was pleasant, but elated and excitable. At other times, he was irritable and barely tolerated me or any other members of staff. This was his baseline: when suffering from psychotic symptoms, he was visibly distracted, responding to unseen stimuli; believing there was a conspiracy to harm him. His paranoid beliefs also stretched to neighbours, whom he spent hours on end examining via security cameras set up in his flat.

Apart from the large amount of electronic equipment - DJ decks, amps, speakers, security cameras and monitors - giving his flat a robotic air, it was in a squalid state. I never saw past his front room, highlighting his mistrust of me, and services as a whole. With the curtains always drawn, and the strong smell of tobacco and sometimes weed evident, such darkness at least hid the flat's overall state of neglect.

Through Mr S's infinitely changeable mood and deep-rooted chaos occasionally shone the real him. During periods of hopefulness, he resolved to stay off the drugs and started to engage more constructively with our team. These spells never lasted though. We worked together sporadically to try and improve his domestic environment and managed to get his toilet unblocked by the local neighbourhood repair team. Unbeknown to me, it had been blocked for several months.

Mr S punched the walls when responding to audio hallucinations. As part of a long-running dispute, he assumed the neighbours were hammering on the walls. Efforts to rectify the resulting large cracks were unfortunately hampered by the presence of Sarah.

Sarah was a mannequin Mr S had somehow acquired from a local charity shop. Lovingly, he dressed her in silky underwear, garish make-up and a variety of wigs. He then topped such design with a sinister-looking black costume and monocle. Placing Sarah just inside his front door - a shadowy figure behind the frosted glass - the sight of her contours was enough to make a burly workman refuse to enter the flat. Making a swift exit, he reputedly said, "Fuck that for a game of soldiers!"

After negotiations with the head of the repair team, a

compromise was reached which required my presence while labourers completed the job of replastering Mr S's walls. I endeavoured to protect them as best I could; Mr S and Sarah behaving with great restraint and charm - Sarah hidden in Mr S's bedroom, accompanied by him throughout most of the visit.

The presence of another lovely creature, his dog Max, was a welcome diversion during *my* official visits and helped to build bridges between us. The sight of Max's 'lipstick' regularly on show whenever I stroked him resulted in some much-needed giggles. The first few years of him living with Mr S - particularly when Mr S was unstable and regularly admitted to hospital – meant us having to find someone to look after Max. Fortunately, our team managed to locate kennels that took great care of him, and were called upon many times.

Mr S's flat was situated on a council estate in Royton, Oldham. As estates go, it was one of the better ones in Oldham. People who used our service were often targets of abuse and exploitation, but such victimisation didn't seem to happen as much here. People nonetheless joked that the estate should be named after the psychiatrist who saw them all regularly.[30] The residents looked out for each other though and were often in each other's flats, which suggested a great camaraderie. Mr S, well known to them all, was considered 'one of us' and they took him under their wing showing great care and concern for his wellbeing.

Royton was always one of my favoured visits, because of the concentration of several charity shops in a small area. I'd often have a ten-minute skive checking out the books and clothes inside. (To ex-colleagues and managers reading this and thinking something along the lines of "Ten minutes, my arse", I can only retort, "Mind your own!")

The charity shops were also favourite haunts of Mr S which, during better times, would have been a source of conversation. At this point, however, my frequenting them only served to breed disapproval from him; catching me out like an employer as he clocked me browsing. There may also have been an element of paranoia though, thinking I was overstepping the mark, monitoring his movements.

After working with Mr S for three years, our relationship became more strained. He was often irritable in my presence. Instead of medication in pill form, he was given depot injections, administered by Kate, a mental health nurse who knew him well. She would accompany me to see Mr S, administer the injection, and then we'd leave. That was the extent of our relationship at this juncture.

During one *solo* visit, Mr S completely lost his rag with me, and I was subjected to a shrill and piercing volley of abuse. His amphetamine use had taken hold and I had inadvertently interrupted a bit of rare sleep on his part upon knocking at the door - the time, three in the afternoon! The subsequent advice from my manager and Mr S's psychiatrist was that I should only visit accompanied by another person. They even considered a change of worker i.e. me.

The situation deteriorated quickly. As part of an ongoing dispute with his neighbour - fuelled largely by Mr S's paranoid delusions - there were threats of violence from both sides. Mr S, upping his battle cry, launched a claw hammer[31] through his neighbour's window - cutting his telephone and broadband wires too in the belief that he was spying on him.

After refusing to speak to us, we immediately set about assembling and authorising an emergency Section - and with it, an admission into hospital. Because of the level of hostility shown to us and his neighbour, we also requested the presence of the local Police. As events unfolded, Mr S refused to move - holding on to Max as if protecting him, plus once again targeting me at the sharp end of his verbal aggression. Eventually, he was restrained and physically forced into the waiting ambulance by Police, who also escorted him to the hospital, leaving us to take care of Max.

As Sections go (never a pleasant experience, however necessary), this was a horrible, messy affair, and I feared my working relationship with Mr S was now irrevocably damaged. The admission would be a turning point in Mr S's life, however.

Parklands House, within Royal Oldham Hospital, was a place where Mr S had spent much of his adult life. And this latest admission would last six months. For the first month, he wasn't entirely with it – neither involved nor consulted about his treatment and activities; spending most of the time in his room (later telling me that he thought the ward psychiatrist - who he knew and generally got on with - was spying on him and hammering on the walls at night, keeping him awake). I kept my distance during this period, as me being in front of him was like a red rag to a bull.

The thawing of our relationship did eventually begin though and came from the simple act of me giving him a Christmas card. The turnaround wasn't immediate, but the week after Christmas he allowed me into his room and told me he was grateful for my card, especially the monkey on the front.

Later that week, during a round of visits with Kate, the mental health nurse, a member of staff told me that Mr S was "in a bad way" asking to see us. I can still picture him answering the door with tears streaming down his face - smudging the makeup and eyeliner that he often experimented with. This was followed by an impromptu hug, and the most open and deeply emotional talk that I had been party to. He disclosed his confusion about what was real, together with his frustration and hopelessness, and his inability to see a "way out". The years of hurt and abuse unravelled before me - such a breakthrough (finally trusting me enough to open up) taking three years. Considering the life that he'd led, and the abuse and damage that he'd suffered, it was hardly surprising.

A factor which contributed towards positive change during this admission was the introduction of a new anti-psychotic medication, Clozaril. Often seen as a last resort,[32] it is used to treat those with severe symptoms of schizophrenia when all other medications have failed. Because of the level of monitoring needed, and Clozaril only being available in pill form at the time, it was originally decided that such medication wasn't appropriate for Mr S, particularly given his sporadic engagement with services. Now that Mr S was in hospital though, the consultant psychiatrist believed that Clozaril was consistent with a better monitoring and treatment programme. It was a long shot for someone with Mr S's history, but it definitely worked for him. His mood, stability and capacity to manage symptoms slowly improved over time.

The most crucial decision during this admission was where Mr S would live after being discharged. Managers at the housing agency were understandably opposed to him returning to his last property. And although he'd inhabited the flat for over a decade – arguably his only *constant* in an otherwise anchorless life - it was clear he'd require supported housing to help prevent the same cycle happening again: drug use, relapse and hospital admission. Fortunately, as time went on, he started to warm to the idea - especially when he realised that a discharge could be expedited if he worked *with* us.

Mr S was initially sent to Mayall Street - a supported housing facility for people with mental health issues, under the legal auspices of a Community Treatment Order.[33] The support he received helped him with practical matters, such as how to structure his day, attend appointments and regularly take his medication. It also helped identify his symptoms and discover ways to cope. Still struggling at this stage, he had another short, hospital admission as a voluntary patient in order to review his medication levels. After that, however, some nine years ago now, he wasn't admitted again. He is adamant that was his last. And I believe him.

When Mayall Street closed, Mr S moved to another supported facility - Highbarn House. While there, he finally relinquished the tenancy to his old Royton flat. Although reluctant to take this step, he recognised that it wasn't financially feasible to keep his present residence *and* the flat as Housing Benefit wouldn't cover both. He also started to fancy the idea of a new start.

Mr S's final move gave him the long-term stability and security that he had previously lacked in his life. He now has tenancy in a house under what is called a Shared Life Scheme. As part of this, he has a specially trained landlord who provides long-term support with tenancy and mental health related issues. The landlord, Darren, has been invaluable assisting Mr S, and goes well beyond his care remit for *all* his tenants. Mr S pays him the ultimate compliment by saying that he is the "father figure" he never had in his life. Since moving into this house, he has truly flowered. And without former impediments – such as chaos and instability - he can now finally be the person he always wanted to.

Mr S is far from the man that he was a mere ten years ago. He trusts people in a way that he couldn't then; his early experiences telling him not to. He now has many close friends - including Aaron, who suffers from similar mental health issues and Jane, a CMHT administration worker, he met at The Beeches. She is the missing piece in his new 'family' being like a "mother figure" to him. For most of us, having friends and trusting relationships is a normal part of our lives - something that we possibly take for granted - but for people like Mr S such connections don't come easily.

The proceeding years have not been without challenges. Mr S has tried numerous voluntary jobs which haven't worked out due to heightened anxiety, leading to increased psychotic symptoms. He still has 'breakthrough' symptoms, and reports that he continuously sees faces in carpets and furniture watching him. He has learned to cope with distraction, mainly watching television and listening to music, and sometimes says that he actually enjoys putting on "a show" for them by singing and dancing.

He still has occasional contact with his sister, but she has her own demons to deal with, including a long-term battle with alcohol dependence. He himself has remained drug-free for a decade now, and occasionally has the odd alcoholic drink without any problems. He reports that staying abstinent has not been too trying, as he still remembers the "nightmare" years when he was in the grip of dependence, and so does not wish to go back there.

The good side of increased independence is that Mr S can now indulge in his love of animals and share his life, once again, with his pets. Max, his dog, stayed with a friend in Royton, but has now passed away. Since then, however, Mr S has kept and lovingly cared for his pet rabbit, H2O, and his gorgeous cat, Larry. His eyes light up when discussing animals and it is these, almost childlike, qualities that define his charm. As well as these precious pets, he still has Sarah, who takes pride of place minus her 'Clockwork Orange' eye monocle.

Mr S is an example of the potential for development and transformation in all of us. He is a success story. There are many survivors out there who also deserve praise for their strength and fortitude, but rarely get it. For him (and those with similar childhood abuse stories), living through such experiences and yet retaining a good chunk of kindness, generosity and humour, is an amazing achievement. Many would have fallen along the way - be languishing in prison, consumed by bitterness, or dead. Avoiding such fates is something that he should be proud of.

Chapter 10 - June

There are no laughs in this chapter. What follows is the story of a sad and tragic, wasted life.

When I started working with June, I realised we were the same age - both in our late thirties. Despite her problems, she was an attractive and warm individual, extremely kind, and no harm to anyone except herself. Her greatest love seemed to be cats. She had many of her own, as well as an army of strays that came to her window to be fed. She named all of them and described their individual characteristics and personalities with glee and humour. Her generosity of spirit was not limited to cats, however. Matty, a friend of mine and postal worker in the Werneth area of Oldham, told me she always used to greet him and his children with a smile, and often gave his kids sweets.

A proper 'rock chick', June dressed mainly in black denim and leather. I could tell when she was feeling good about her world as she embellished her hair with purple streaks or wore colourful scarves. During these times she was very talkative, with a sense of humour accentuating her wry take on life. When she was low in mood though, it was harder to get responses from her. I tended to avoid troubling issues when this happened and turned the conversation to music and clubs that she used to frequent. We talked about Jilly's and The Banshee, in Manchester - clubs we had both been to. After breaking the ice, I was able to turn her attention to pertinent problems in her life.

~ ~ ~

These 'keys to engagement' helped to build rapport, common interests and - hopefully - trust. Through my own passions (music, football and sport in general) I found out what makes other people tick. Politics best avoided, but otherwise anything and everything - me being adaptable. Music is an especially good topic for me, as I tend to 'dip my toe' into all sorts of genres, so can usually find common ground. My support for the great Carlisle United (The Cumbrians) is often a source of hilarity, but manages to solicit its way towards a 'therapeutic relationship'. Out of the corner of my eye during a particularly frosty visit to one man who displayed a deep mistrust of mental health services, I spotted a painting on his wall of DJ, John Peel. Once I'd eulogised about the influence of this great man, and how much I loved the painting, the atmosphere warmed up nicely. So you see, sometimes it's just about finding that elusive 'way in'. Bloody social work - it ain't rocket science!

~ ~ ~

After seeing June a couple of times, it became obvious that she suffered from extreme mood swings and that her life was chaotic. Her past and present diagnoses - severe anxiety with periods of clinical depression and Emotionally Instable Personality Disorder - all pointed to this. Prior to her referral to my CMHT team, she had presented herself at A&E at the Royal Oldham Hospital on numerous occasions, disclosing suicidal ideation, low mood and hopelessness. During her last visit she received clinical treatment following an overdose. Suicide attempts and self-harm in the form of cutting her arms were mentioned in her risk history.

These characteristics and risks were common in people we worked with at The Beeches - a building near the centre of Oldham where part of the CMHT was based. What wasn't evidenced at this point, however - just below the surface - were the issues that caused such distress. And the clue to these would only become visible later; slowly but surely, like peeling an onion to reveal new layers once trust is established.

After our initial assessment meetings, I suggested a referral to clinical psychology. June was initially resistant, saying that she had seen a counsellor before and it "didn't do any good". At our next meeting though, having thought through her options, she agreed to give it a try. At The Beeches we had a clinical psychologist who was a vital resource in the understanding of, and methods of working with, certain people that used our service.[34] As well as direct, therapeutic work and a range of talking therapies,[35] with patients, the psychologists were invaluable in an advisory role to CMHT practitioners. They were especially indispensable when we felt stuck - not knowing quite what to do; a common feeling when dealing with people in the throes of complex issues.

I have seen cognitive behavioural therapy (CBT) work well with people who have overwhelming anxiety, helping to reframe their thoughts and fears which are often based on 'What if…?' worst-case scenarios, by looking at alternative ways of thinking. In June's case, there was clearly the need to look deeper and utilise the techniques of cognitive analytic therapy (CAT) in order to examine the causes of her distress from the past. (It is a fascinating area, and worthy of deeper investigation into its general concepts, rather than the superficial 'Idiots Guide' I have outlined.)

Those undergoing such therapy often need increased support during and after, as opening up and delving into painful memories can result in *more* distress over the short term, as was the case with June. At The Beeches, in a flood of tears, she started to discuss her estranged relationship with her mother, and it became evident to me that this was one of the root causes of her present distress. After sending letter after letter with no reply, she decided to visit her mother in a relatively prosperous neighbourhood to the south of Manchester, where she ironically practised as a counsellor. Her mother answered the door, but told June that she didn't want any contact with her, and asked her not to call again. The reasons behind this absolute rejection never became clear.

As June began to open up, she gave me more clues though. Reports in her file indicated heroin addiction, and she confirmed this. She also disclosed that her urge to use it again had increased recently, yet she had the insight to realise she required help. I referred her to the local drug treatment agency - still within the NHS in Oldham at this time - for support with relapse prevention. It would help her understand her personal triggers for using drugs and teach her how to deal with them. I asked one of our CMHT support workers, Danna, to do some short-term work - first, accompanying her to the initial appointments, as June had shown reluctance and anxiety about attending these alone. This worked well, and while there she was referred to a Structured Day Service, also run by Drug and Alcohol Services, similar to the Lifeline project where I'd worked previously.

During this period, I discovered that June had a daughter she was keen to re-establish a better relationship with. She attended college in Manchester, having largely been brought up by June's mother. Although it was a strained relationship, there was at least *some* contact. June proudly showed me pictures of them together, with her daughter looking very much like a younger version of her. June's need to compensate for what she perceived as her failings as a mother were huge, and this often took the form of extravagant presents and gifts; money to her daughter which she obviously couldn't afford.

It soon became evident that June's personal finances were in a chaotic state. With the help of Danna, she was introduced to a Citizens Advice Bureau debt advice worker, however, who helped her identify and prioritise her debts, plus establish manageable repayment plans. With her consent, the local authority in Oldham took responsibility for her financial affairs under an appointeeship arrangement, which enabled her to have enough to live on whilst reducing her debt. With the help of this extensive package of care, June reached a level of confidence not previously seen and avoided further drug use in the interim. However, as one issue seemed under control, another one became problematic.

In her flat, I noticed a picture of June taken around ten years before. She was barely recognisable due to her size and general appearance. June told me that her weight had always been "a problem" and had severely fluctuated throughout her lifetime. In the picture, she was much larger and would have been classed as clinically obese. Her present appearance, by contrast, was considered healthy and normal. The reality behind her surface looks was far from a picture of health though. Over a period of several meetings with Danna and I, June disclosed her binge eating habits and use of laxatives. After eating large amounts of snacks - usually cakes and biscuits - she would take vast amounts of laxatives to *purge* her body of the food.

Using laxatives in this way is a compensatory behaviour exhibited by sufferers of bulimia, who use them to cope with the subsequent anxiety they feel after binge eating. This becomes a dangerous cycle, of course, as the tolerance to laxatives increases and thus *more* need to be taken to have any effect. Unlike anorexia, which is characterised by extreme weight loss, bulimia isn't easily spotted as sufferers present with normal body weight and can even be overweight or bloated in appearance. It was impossible, therefore, for us to know how long June had had this disorder. I had been working with her for a year, but had been none the wiser.

Initially flippant and someone who'd rather gloss over things, June seemed to be in denial regarding the damage she was doing to herself. Slowly her defences came down though, and after much coaxing and persuasion, she recognised she had a problem; with the motivation to do something about it improving incrementally. (My earlier training at Lifeline Drugs Project on motivational interviewing came in useful here, unlike most mainstream, social work theory which I found to be largely useless in practice.)

We accessed an emergency appointment with June's GP at the local practice in Werneth. They did the relevant assessments and referred her to the Specialist Eating Disorder Service in Salford. I accompanied June to this appointment, yet nothing could quite prepare me for the experience of being inside the waiting room there.

The service was located in an old Edwardian building, in a residential area of Salford. The waiting room itself was small and cramped, and overwhelmingly populated by incredibly self-conscious young girls with emaciated frames and large, sunken eyes. They may not have been as young as they looked. Everyone was silent. No one made eye contact. All were focused - staring intently at the pattern of the carpet. The feeling of not knowing where to put your eyes was unbearable. And the intense claustrophobia was reinforced by the layout of the chairs - inanely situated in a ring so we all faced each other. This may be my memory serving me incorrectly, exaggerating the sheer unease that I felt, but I'm sure it was like that. If so, I can only hope that the layout has been altered since, allowing more privacy.

The level of anxiety in the room was too much for June, and she indicated that she was stepping outside for some "fresh air"; code for a cigarette. I joined her - this being the perfect time for a fag, even though it was against the rules and would certainly have been frowned upon by management and some of my colleagues.[36]

The appointment itself felt like a relief, compared to the experience of waiting. Despite this, it was still an ordeal for June and she became tearful while disclosing the full extent of her eating disorder. I was taken aback as she told the doctor how many laxative pills she typically swallowed on a daily basis. (It's not uncommon for sufferers to ingest fifty pills a day.) In a professional and understanding manner, the doctor assessed the degree of June's disorder and decided that it didn't require *immediate* admission into a specialist ward and could be treated with regular, outpatient appointments.

The treatment included a gradual and monitored reduction in laxative usage until complete abstinence was reached. Advice from a dietician, plus regular counselling which addressed her psychological dependence on binge eating and purging, were also part of the care package. And on a more practical level, June received pads and special incontinence sheets when she reported problems with diarrhoea and accidents while in bed.

Following this coordinated programme, June achieved something which had previously been elusive: a form of stability in her life. And she showed great motivation in wanting to change her life for the better. With real iron determination, she attended the day service regularly and became a mentor in activities, including climbing, having responsibility for the monitoring and teaching of others. She excelled in physical activities, and I often saw her out jogging. Although heartening to observe, I still had the nagging feeling that she dealt in extremes (associated with her eating disorder) rather than moderate and balanced exercise designed to keep her fit.

Despite the misgivings we had, however, it was clear that June was mentally sharper than she had been, particularly with a good support network around her. It is difficult to decide *when* to put an end to someone's involvement with mental health services, but such decisions do have to be made. Services are a scarce resource, much in demand. Because of the inevitable, post-services risks, it is always emphasised that people can *re-refer* if they feel vulnerable or in need.

Looking back, it pleases me just how much we were able to provide for June over a two-year period; the ease of access and breadth of services available back then. This would certainly not be the case now. Many resources have been withdrawn, or are accompanied by charges. And the pathways to various services are often complicated by Kafkaesque commissioning and rationing. The contrast between then and now shines a brutal light on how much has been stripped from the most vulnerable in society. Austerity and cuts in funding over the last eleven years have put paid to the notion that those at the top have compassion.

After her case was closed by our team, I still saw June intermittently - out running, as mentioned. She was still into her exercise regime at this point, and proudly described her impressive climbing feats.[37] I remember her light-hearted quip, "Eh, I'm no woose me, y'know", and I could only agree. It was always lovely to see her, and she was never anything less than pleasant and warm.

For six months, I didn't lay eyes on June. Rumours began to surface though regarding her escalating drug use. Coincidentally, I was working with a woman called Jane with equally complex problems, who happened to live next door to June. She wasn't aware that I'd previously worked with June, but told me about her neighbour's regular contact with a well-known pimp; a man who allegedly forced women to prostitute themselves to fund his drug habit. She also said that June was in the grip of a spiralling, heroin addiction - selling her body for pitiful amounts to men who abused her. And the last, final bit of information certainly rang true: that she always made sure her cats were "fed and watered" despite neglecting herself.

I was in a state of shock when I eventually saw her.

I was in a bar in Oldham having a drink after work. There weren't many in there, this being a weeknight - just a few 'teatime tipplers' like myself. June walked through the bar, but didn't stop to have a drink. She seemed to be looking for someone, but couldn't find them. I'm good at facial recognition and usually spot a familiar mug before it's seen me. This was a face I barely recognised though, given that it now had a spider's web tattoo covering half of it. The black ink added to an aura of degradation, and the rest of her face was grey, hollowed and worn. Her shuffling gait, avoidance of eye contact and clothes that had seen better days - now hanging off her worryingly slim frame - all gave clues to her present predicament, and a state of mind that was beyond hoping for better.

I didn't get the chance to speak to June that day. By the time I recognised her, she was gone. I remember needing time to internalise and reconcile this image with the person I had known, however.

Not long after this episode, I saw her while walking through the town centre, near Oldham Magistrates (now closed). My conversation with her was brief. She told me that she'd just been in court. I did not ask why. I didn't need to. And she wasn't in the mood to expand on the reason why. Desperate to find something to say, I asked if she'd attended drug services recently. She shrugged, indicated that she hadn't and replied, "What's the point?"

Her whole manner implied defeat. She had given up. Her spark had gone out.

It was the last time I would speak with June. I heard about her regular court appearances through the Oldham Chronicle. Soon after, in 2013, I read that she'd received a three-year Anti-Social Behaviour Order (ASBO), forbidding her to 'loiter' in the Arkwright Street area following multiple arrests (the exact count six, for soliciting over the last twelve months).

June was found dead in her flat a month later.

~ ~ ~

Writing about June, and knowing about many others who have similar, tragic endings, reinforces my anger over how society treats those dependent on drugs. The prohibition of drugs and criminalisation of prostitution enables pimps and gangs to exploit users and sex workers, thereby bestowing power and wealth upon the ruthless. Those at the bottom of this ladder risk their lives every day to feed their habit. And the current laws, futile 'War on Drugs' etc., do not (and will not) stop drug use and the crimes committed in order to pay for it.

The drugs trade remains unregulated, resulting in users not knowing the strength of the drugs they take, and what other substances might be mixed in; the product 'cut' at every level of the drugs trade ladder. This inevitably leads to overdoses, deaths, and the ill health of those pale, ghostlike figures who inhabit the streets of our towns and cities. And somewhat perversely, in my experience, I have found that the majority of those in charge of handling this situation - the Police and the legal profession - agree that we *must* radically alter the way drugs, crime and prostitution are dealt with.

I'm not saying that June could have been saved. She was deeply damaged. And her self-destructive urges may have led to her death whatever the legal context. However, I *am* saying that the present laws governing drugs and prostitution served to provide the boot which trampled her face deeper into the gutter and left her with nowhere else to go. The emphasis needs to be shifted from criminalisation to treatment, along with safe places for those engaging in such activity. I fear that we are now as far away from this mature approach as we have ever been though. And many more Junes will die in the meantime.

~ ~ ~

Writing this chapter has been hard, as I desperately want to do justice to the memory of June. I only found out about her death and subsequent funeral from Matty, the postal worker mentioned at the start of this piece. We have both reminisced about her on occasions and - as well as others - remembered her as the lovely, kind human being that she was. It is a crying shame that she never quite knew how appreciated she was and the regard in which she was held by those who really knew her.

Chapter 11 - Waiting Rooms

Time spent waiting for appointments was an inevitable, often irritating, part of my job as a social worker. The job could be time-pressured, with deadlines needing to be adhered to, plus reports and contracts for care providers prioritised. When minutes and hours were squandered waiting for appointments - however important - it therefore added to the stress of the job.

On the upside, I developed a well-honed 'First impressions antennae' and got the feel of a place from how I was treated while waiting; an instinctive gauge that was rarely wrong. At nursing and residential homes - seeing people on my caseload as a Best Interest Assessor[38] - the 'Brew rule' was instrumental in forming initial impressions. I often travelled long distances, using public transport, and if the offer of a cup of tea/coffee on arrival wasn't forthcoming then I was less than happy. As a visiting professional I had considerable sway over each home's finances when it came to the decision of whether to commission rooms there. And so, if this basic courtesy wasn't extended, then it made me wonder how residents were treated i.e. those with a less powerful voice.

Olfactory cues - even the faintest whiff of urine - also influenced my impression of a home. I understand that it is not easy to achieve 'aroma perfection' when there are residents who are doubly incontinent, and that it demands the most regimented of cleaning regimes, but standards have to be high even when there are considerable time and staffing constraints.[39]

The larger, institutional waiting rooms gave a gloomy impression of the services therein. And the chance of being offered a brew in places like these was minimal to none. In the last chapter, I described the tension inside a waiting room at an Eating Disorder Service. Even to an 'outsider', or paid accompaniment to the service user, the stilted and oppressive atmosphere was deeply affecting. Usually, when waiting with someone, my cheerful and reassuring small talk came to the fore. This was not the time to discuss the reason we were here; such formal talk would happen behind closed doors, during the appointment. The person with me was often nervous ahead of baring their inner demons to others, and so I did my best to comfort them and instil motivational reassurances that they were 'doing the right thing'. The hushed atmosphere of this particular waiting room made it a bit harder though, as its claustrophobic imprint seemed to suck the air out of our lungs, leaving only a foreboding silence.

If that was the most self-conscious waiting room that I've ever encountered, then the most depressing one was inside The Department for Work and Pensions (DWP), Albert Bridge House, Manchester. People were assessed here to determine whether their disabilities matched the benefits they received; be it ESA (Employment Support Allowance) or PIP (Personal Independence Payment), which has now replaced the Disabled Living Allowance. The building itself, an imposing, grey concrete monolith, set the tone before witnessing the shabby, utilitarian interior. Everything, including the nailed-down seating, had a grubby, overused feel to it. I usually exited the building feeling like the remnants of this grubbiness were still with me. Perhaps the building's vicinity, next to Deansgate's canal, was no coincidence. I often wondered how many people had used the nearby water for a quick wash, or for sadder and graver reasons. No one wanted to be in that building or waiting room. The people there - society's poorest - were routinely summoned to justify their benefits and means of existing, and so the aura of resentment was palpable.

The minutes before an appointment were unnerving as claimants usually felt like they were being watched. The reputation surrounding the place came from verifiable stories concerning disabled claimants allegedly 'caught out' for standing up *too* quickly or walking *too* easily to the toilet before an interview. The 'Bridge Street Limp', describing those with physical disabilities who allegedly exaggerate their injuries on the street leading up to the building, is now part of Manchester folklore.

Far too much of my time as a social worker was taken up helping people with DWP forms in relation to benefits; time which could have been used more productively for therapeutic purposes. PIP and ESA forms are long, laborious affairs and soul-destroying in their repetition of questions. I usually filled in the forms myself, as other agencies - such as the Citizens Advice Bureau - were completely overburdened, with crazy waiting times. Many hours were also spent writing supportive, professional letters or completing assessments over the phone with DWP assessors.

During these calls, I was 'reassured' that the assessor was appropriately qualified (often a registered nurse), but my immediate, unspoken reaction was, "Well, you're not nursing *now* are you?" I could speculate as to *why* they are still registered - after all, I wouldn't expect to call myself a social worker if I'm not actually practising in the profession. So, however pleasant the caller seemed, I maintained a healthy dose of scepticism regarding their motives - not least because I knew they were paid *double* the wages of actual nurses; those using their skills fruitfully, rather than indulging in cold assessments on behalf of the government.

I say this not to castigate civil servants working inside the DWP. There are, inevitably, good and bad, just like at other institutions. It is, though, my assertion that a high-level, cynical mistrust of society's poor and disabled - which results in them *constantly* having to justify themselves in relation to welfare payments – doesn't help at all. And I am resolute in saying that during my time as a social worker, I neither worked with 'freeloaders' nor 'scroungers'. To utilise our services they had to present with very *real* and profound, deep-seated problems. It is my belief, therefore, that our professional assessments should be trusted without the need for more exhaustive information.[40]

I dreaded appointments at Albert Bridge House. They rarely resulted in a withdrawal of benefits for those I assisted, but did epitomise the state's woeful treatment of those on society's bottom rung. Welfare was no longer a right, it seemed, for those who had fallen on hard times, but a 'charitable' contribution to be accounted for.

By contrast, there were appointments that I rather looked forward to - namely, regular visits to the local Sexual Health Clinic. I accompanied a woman who was HIV+ to the clinic in Oldham and always weirdly enjoyed the experience. I can honestly say that I've never met a better staff team.[41] (The service was outsourced during this period and was taken over by the Virgin brand. Yes, that's right, the Virgin Sexual Health Centre. You couldn't make it up.) Although prone to extreme mood swings and extremely challenging behaviour, my client was always received with respect, understanding and - above all - good humour. I suppose if you make a living inspecting potentially diseased genitals all day, then you need a pretty grounded character and sense of humour. I imagine this team's Christmas nights out were a riot.

The SHC waiting room was always a source of fascination to me - an experience obviously made easier as it wasn't *me* sitting there waiting to have my nether regions inspected. The stage was perfectly set for conjecture about those present - many of whom exuded an obvious sense of embarrassment, shame, and the desire not to be recognised. While waiting, I often let my imagination roam over the situations around me: the disapproving mother, with her tense daughter; the two gay guys, who dealt with their nerves through loud, raucous humour; and the strange bloke in the corner.

I'm surprised there hasn't been a sitcom based on the comings and goings in such a place. It seemed to have it all – every character, every demographic. I realise it may sound somewhat callous, taking enjoyment from others' misery, but in my defence we all need something to pass the time while waiting.

Appointments that tested my patience the most were always ward rounds on mental health units. The psychiatrists undoubtedly had many skills and talents, but time management wasn't one of them. On average, if they started half an hour late, then I felt lucky. There was, in among this, the decision of *where* to wait; most wards not possessing obvious, signposted areas, and if tucked away, there was the realistic fear that you'd be forgotten about. So this, or waiting in the corridor like a spare part - the object of much curiosity from the rest of the patients – were usually the options.

Due to the starry-eyed notion of maintaining confidentiality, we were encouraged not to reveal the identity of the person we were waiting for. The evasiveness of my replies thus caused *more* suspicion, to the point that a relapse in certain patients' paranoid symptoms was inevitable. "You a copper then?" was one of many enquiries I had to broach.

During these times, I sensed the atmosphere of the ward, and soon noticed potential areas of conflict. Smoking was banned on psychiatric units (and in mental health facilities) in July 2008 – one year after "enclosed work places" - and much of the interaction and tension between patients and nursing staff revolved around this. To compensate, staff took patients out for regular smoking breaks, but the timing of these still gave room for complaint. (I understand the rationale behind such regulation in terms of reducing the effects of passive smoking, but as a smoker myself, I also sympathise with patients as the *worst* time to limit smoking is during a mental health setback.)

A large element of addiction, especially smoking, is psychological and habitual effects-wise, rather than purely physiological, so nicotine patches are insufficient. I confess to missing, during these later years, the offer of a fag and a chat outside in order to strategically diffuse conflict situations. Less controversial, de-escalation techniques are obviously available, but I do miss this one!

Wards were often characterised by their sheer busyness, with staff overburdened by increasing demands and priorities. Therefore, even making a brew for myself as a visitor was a fraught mission and invariably meant having to bother staff for keys to the kitchen. I mostly tended to go without therefore, as all that was available was decaf, which - for a caffeine addict - is pointless anyway. You would have to be pretty selfish and thick-skinned to apply the 'Brew rule' to a busy ward though.

The pressure on Community Psychiatric Outpatient Departments is the equivalent to that on wards, but is a different experience altogether. The sheer number of people that NHS psychiatrists have as part of their caseloads is overwhelming. I would be hard-pushed to recognise the faces of these individuals, never mind their names if in the hundreds. Having worked with the same client group in the same area for many years, I knew many of those waiting, and it was usually pleasant catching up with such people.

There *were* conversations, however, that veered away from small talk and challenged the very notion of privacy. Once, I was sat in the Outpatients department with Jim, a patient prone to manic episodes, which meant he became loud and disinhibited. It is a common complaint that certain medications - especially higher doses of anti-depressants - can cause sexual dysfunction. So, it was perhaps expected when he irritably declared to me, and the whole of the room, "I just can't cum, Richard!" However much I tried to reassure him that we would talk about this issue with the psychiatrist, it became impossible to stem the immediate consensus (and similar grievances) in the room, much to the bemusement of an older woman and her relatives trying to mind their own business.

Most of us have waited in A&E at some point in our lives. Working in mental health, this tended to be *after* typical 9 to 5 office hours, once all other options had been exhausted. Incidents included the Police having to attend Section 136 Suites. Meant to be 'places of safety' where detained people wait in order to be assessed (under the Mental Health Act), the reality of these suites is that they are inevitably fraught with high tension and the potential for further incidents. I witnessed many, including one occasion where a Police officer was physically assaulted by a young man who called him "the devil wrapped in pigskin"; his fists raining down on him. Security staff helped restrain the aggressor amid screaming and shouting. People detained under s136 tended to be the most mentally ill, or the most violent - *both*, if you were unlucky. Waiting for the appropriate clinical attention was torturous, and the relief at being able to leave was immense.

What of the poor members of the public who waited to meet *me*, you may ask? I can only be evasive and defensive in response. The waiting environment and atmosphere was largely out of my control, and mostly influenced by the calibre of staff present. The administrative staff were usually warm and competent; a real credit given their underpaid and undervalued roles. Certain individuals, however (I shall keep their identities anonymous), had the expression and aura of something - if added to milk - you wouldn't pour on your cornflakes; gladly trading it for dog piss.

I have always found that waiting in places such as A&E makes me appreciate the work of the staff there. I am in awe of their capacity for patience and resilience, and will state the obvious by saying they need more support. A clap each Thursday night during lockdown is nowhere near enough. It is difficult not to feel useless though in situations where others are overworked. You just sit there wondering what to do. Too many hours have been spent like this over the last 32 years. And it is an experience that I do not miss.

Chapter 12 - Mr W

During my time with the Care Management and Review Team[42] - the *last* team I was a part of in the course of my 'illustrious' career - I worked with Mr W.

While reading the historical assessments of him, I had a sense of foreboding - especially when it came to risk. Mr W was on the Sex Offenders Register and had been habitual in his offending behaviour throughout his adult life. His forensic history was long and well documented: the majority of incidents, him exposing himself to others - sometimes while masturbating in public places, other times through the window of his house. Generally, when people think of 'sex offenders' their perception is of an assault on a person in the form of a direct physical attack. Although this wasn't the case with Mr W, his victims were still damaged by such incidents, and I certainly don't wish to minimise his crimes.

The contrast between reading these records and actually seeing him - a small, fragile, unhealthy, vulnerable old man - was huge, however. Due to kidney failure, Mr W had a colostomy bag which he regularly emptied into his toilet, opposite the kitchen in the narrow corridor leading to his living room. The vinegary stench of urine was overpowering; the pungent smell also due to his dog, a little Jack Russell, having "accidents". The dog became an increasing problem, fond of me as it was - its affection displayed by sniffing and licking, then a volley of snapping bites. Around the time of my third visit, 'the gobby little bastard' - as I liked to call him - outside the hearing range of Mr W's world, was successful in his pursuit of me, subsequently biting me and piercing the skin on my left hand. After an emergency visit to the local 'Walk In' Health Centre, and a most undignified tetanus injection, future visits to Mr W's came with the proviso that 'gobby' bastard would be banished to Mr W's bedroom.

With little trust of mental health services and his care, Mr W bitterly complained about the "deadening", sedative effects of the anti-psychotic injections he received every fortnight. Administered by the community mental health nurses at a local clinic, the injections were a substitute for oral medication; prescribed to forgetful individuals or those who were 'non-compliant'. When Phil[43] (the support worker in attendance) and I suggested an appointment with Dr Mason, Mr W's psychiatrist, in order to discuss changing the strength or frequency of the injection, this was dismissed out of hand by Mr W. In no uncertain terms, he told us quite vociferously that we were "all the same" and "out to control me".

He often became loud and angry when discussing his mental health treatment. Minimising the consequences of his behaviour, he shouted, "There's nothing wrong with nudity. It's natural - right back to Adam 'n' Eve. I don't know what all the fuss is about wi' you lot!"

When it was pointed out, "That's all well and good, but you don't give your victims any choice, do you", he stuck to his view belligerently.

Diagnosed with chronic obstructive pulmonary disease, not helped by decades of smoking, Mr W only spoke when he could get his breath between wheezes and rasping coughs. At its worst, this prevented him from speaking for a while and sounded - especially on the phone - like a heavy breather with suspect intent. Curiously enough, this wasn't one of his recorded crimes.

Despite trying to de-escalate his outbursts, Mr W would

sometimes regale us with a heated lecture on psychiatric treatment and its social control role in society. He was articulate and seemed to have some knowledge of anti-psychiatry theory from writers such as Goffman, Foucault and RD Laing.[44] To an extent, he was right. We were attempting to control his more damaging behaviour, and ultimately there was a power relationship, as we had the power to place him in hospital against his wishes if need be. The social context of mental health problems must also be emphasised though, as I hope is evident throughout this book.

I reject wild, libertarian claims regarding the 'myth of mental illness' and am confident that our actions are needed in the interests of 'the common good', however subjective this notion may be. I also suspect that deep down Mr W realised that treatment was in his best interests, as shown by his actions which often contradicted his theoretical stance. When he saw Dr Mason, he was invariably warm and courteous, and on one occasion asked for an increase in the strength of his depot / slow-release medication as he often became distressed during the short window before his next injection. Whether this reflected great insight gained through decades of illness wasn't clear, but it did show that despite his protestations he knew there was something wrong.

Diagnosed with chronic schizophrenia, Mr W's symptoms included aural hallucinations e.g. neighbours or local residents banging on the walls and windows, plus paranoid ideas about people acting in a hostile way ('persecutory delusions' in psychiatric terms). I witnessed his visible distress from the "bloody banging" despite no evidence from my own ears to back it up. During these episodes, he became irritable and was more likely to indulge in offending behaviour, reports suggest.

Mr W's delusional ways also gave credence to the idea that his neighbour was spying on him, as well as hammering on the walls. An old, rather frail lady, she was surprisingly understanding and sympathetic when it came to Mr W's lewd and obnoxious acts. Expressing her concern one day, she reported hearing lots of shouting from his flat. In this instance, his medication was increased, which seemed to introduce a period of greater calm.

Other incidents confirmed that Mr W *did* have a degree of control over his behaviour, rather than it being solely determined by his psychotic state. Because of his many offences though, he had a long history of involvement with the criminal justice system. Having extensive contact with his probation worker, who was largely at a loss about what to do, I discovered that Mr W's offending behaviour tended to cease when he was given a suspended sentence (the threat of a *custodial* sentence perhaps hammering home the seriousness of his actions). No other interventions seemed to work; sexual offender group work and one-to-one sessions explored, but ineffective.

I compiled a report for a pre-sentencing panel after Mr W once again exposed himself through the window of his flat. In it, I included details about his mental health condition and treatment, together with recommendations. I also included some forensic history, such as offences when he was younger and more mobile e.g. 'Masturbation in public places'. Unfortunately, I mistakenly left out an 'l', so it read: 'Masturbation in *pubic* places'. This was fortunately spotted by the highly-amused probation worker before being submitted to the judge.

~ ~ ~

People with horrific and long-term, forensic history are often fascinating conundrums (if you're into that sort of thing). And the popularity of real crime dramas and documentaries suggests I'm not alone in having such morbid curiosity. Whether criminal actions are caused by mental illness, or the result of flawed and damaged personalities, is at the forefront of debate. Simplified, the question becomes: 'Mad or Bad?'

Early in my career, I visited a man in a secure hospital designed for those with forensic histories. While waiting to see him, I chatted with a patient who struck me as affable and extremely helpful. Later, when I learnt about this individual's chilling, forensic history of abhorrent paedophilia-related crimes, I felt deflated, gullible and shocked. In studies of psychopathy, those diagnosed often exhibit cultivated and calculated charm – not something I ever saw in Mr W, as I don't believe he tried to charm or fool us. On the contrary, I felt that he was sincere in what he said, however flawed he was. I didn't get the sense that he was a misanthropist either – someone with a deep-seated hatred of humanity. Most of the time, in fact, he was a pleasure to be with (always greeting us as "Lad", an Oldham custom between men of all ages). He had a lively sense of humour too.

Although I wouldn't say Mr W was guarded, he did only give a limited amount away, and I never felt on solid-enough ground to claim that I *really* knew him. Our support team, from a practical standpoint, encouraged him to improve the cleanliness of his flat - suggesting that the urine-sodden carpet be replaced - and he did, to be fair, hire a cleaner for its upkeep from an agency we often commissioned. It was hoped that, as well as improving his living conditions and the general aroma of the place, such a simple change would benefit his breathing.

He had previously said that he'd already paid someone to do this, despite clear evidence to the contrary, but after asking him to consider 'changing' said cleaner, I visited a fortnight later and found the flat transformed. A new carpet had been laid, having the desired effect of massively reducing ammonia levels, and the whole flat looked *proper* spick and span. Mr W explained, with a beaming smile, that he'd employed "a mate" to replace the carpet and had hired a 'new' cleaner. He subsequently told us, quite openly, that his new cleaner was also the "receptionist" at the massage parlour in Oldham town centre (which he frequented regularly). Whether other services were available as part of this new care package was unknown. Also unknown was the amount he was paying said individual. When asked, he was evasive and replied with a different figure each time.[45] There was no *direct* evidence of financial exploitation, but we had no right of access to Mr W's account even though we suspected shady goings-on.

We only had a limited, partial picture of Mr W's past. The information gleaned from historical files held few details beyond the fact that he'd had a 'difficult childhood'. There is increasing awareness concerning the prevalence of childhood sexual abuse among those who suffer psychotic symptoms in later life. And my experience working with such individuals bears this out. Evidence also reveals that individuals sexually abused as children often engage in abusive relationships as adults - sometimes as the abuser. We need to be careful how we interpret behavioural patterns and not jump to conclusions, as the majority of those who suffer childhood abuse *do not* complete this cycle by abusing others. Our concern about Mr W was valid though in terms of his past, but we had no solid corroboration.

In one of his better moods, Mr W would let us in a little and talk about his childhood and youth. He'd usually rattle on about happy memories - sharing anecdotes about various warehouses and factories he'd had the pleasure of working inside. He also mentioned doing a stint on a farm in quite glowing terms, but his special love was working with horses; the glint in his eye when discussing this giving us a slightly uneasy feeling. There was much conjecture between Phil and I over whether there were more sordid reasons for this special affection; Mr W's small stature - no more than five feet tall - adding to speculation as to why the poor little Shetland ponies were his favourites.

On occasions, Mr W pushed the limits during visits. One instance involved us being greeted by him and pornography courtesy of his TV set. I asked him to turn it off, which he did without any fuss, but in defence of the minimally-clad young women cavorting on screen Mr W claimed that they were "nice lasses". The fact that the 'nicer' they were, the more viewers were coaxed into phoning up, prompting a further shedding of clothes - thereby incurring massive charges - didn't seem to alter his opinion.

Other situations included exhibiting pornographic material during visits. And I can only imagine that these were calculated plans design to shock naïve and unworldly souls. Female staff were often targeted in this way - something which had to be taken seriously and assessed in terms of risk. In fact, because of this, it was decided that Mr W should only have male members of staff visiting, given that females were his intended victims. On one occasion, in an illuminating and chilling way, he disclosed that he got a "thrill" from his actions - seeing the shock on people's faces.

It is difficult to write about those who sexually offend. They are, understandably, some of the most hated figures in society. It is also true, as a social worker dealing with the worst forms of human action, that we become inured to the horror that such behaviour invokes. Seeking to *understand* an individual who commits vile acts does not equate to excusing such behaviour though. If we are not to react with traditional, knee-jerk 'stone age' morality as tabloid press proponents do (lock them up and 'throw away the key'), then something fresh and innovative must be put on the table; these types of people needing to be worked with by *somebody* and not only in a monitoring capacity, thus keeping society safe. It is also an uncomfortable truth that people who commit heinous acts are rarely the monsters one imagines. Instead, they are complex and flawed human beings not too dissimilar to ourselves and seldom rotten to the core.

Most of my former managers would agree that keeping vital paperwork up to date, such as risk assessments, was not my strong point. However, as they were needed regularly for Mr W because of ongoing risks, files were up to date on the sad occasion when he succumbed to chronic health problems and died four years ago.

A complex individual whose character and actions often contradicted each other, most of the time Mr W was affable and warm - in stark contrast to the repellent nature of his crimes. In many ways, he defied understanding. And I still have more questions than answers about those who commit such heinous, but sometimes sordid and pathetic, crimes.

Chapter 13 - Mr L

Mr L has been a colourful part of my life for over ten years now. He's one of those unique and irascible characters who, once met, is never forgotten. I still see him regularly, and genuinely hope this will remain the case for a long time. He has reviewed this chapter with me, refining some of the weightier points, and has not been shy in coming forward with corrections about particular details of his life.

When Mr L's case was allocated to me, he was already well known to the Community Mental Health Team at The Beeches. Practically all the staff had had some experience of working with him, including admin personnel who answered his many impassioned phone calls.

I was five years into my job as a social worker when I first met him and enjoyed the team dynamics of the CMHT. The Beeches crew were a familiar sight at The Ashton Arms on Fridays, after a gruelling week. A wonderful, real ale hostelry in the centre of Oldham, regulars there were well-accustomed to the fact that psychiatric nurses tended to be pretty loud after a few drinks. Looking back, this was my favourite period working in social care. Feeling established enough to know that I was doing a good job and was well supported by colleagues with a similar outlook and value system, meant that the working atmosphere was largely consensual and warm. And when a team works well together, lame and contrived attempts at teambuilding elsewhere are put into perspective i.e. the dustbin of my memories.

Danna, a support worker at The Beeches, was instrumental in creating my happy memories over this period. It was during her 30th birthday night out that I was introduced to my future wife,

Natalie; Danna subsequently gaining the title of 'work wife', as we worked many hours together supporting different, challenging people (including the subject of this chapter). She has been a constant source of hilarity, insults and jip ever since.

~ ~ ~

My relationship with Mr L did not start off on a particularly great, harmonious footing. I was initially asked to see him as part of a one-off visit in relation to his request for a cleaner. After visiting his flat and assessing his case, I saw no reason why he couldn't do this himself or pay for a private cleaner. I gave him the number of the agency that we often used, but told him that he'd have to fund this from out of his disability benefits. He was indignant at what he perceived to be a snub and expressed this in no uncertain terms.

On the next occasion we met, I was required to assess the state of his mental health as he'd been allocated to me. Concerns had been relayed to the team regarding his wild, disinhibited behaviour. Mr L had a long-term diagnosis and was bi-polar[46] - a condition once known as manic depression. He'd been arguing with strangers in the town centre, speaking and singing to himself, and admin staff had reported an increase in erratic phone calls - clear warning signs that he was experiencing the manic stage of his illness. After briefly seeing him at his flat, I assessed the situation as *beyond* the support services' risk level in terms of managing his behaviour. The last resort of a Mental Health Assessment[47] in pursuance of hospital admission had to be authorised therefore.

A psychiatrist, GP, AMHP (Approved Mental Health Professional) and I assembled at the front of his flat and knocked on the door, but there was no answer. He did respond to a phone call, but it was clear that he wasn't home and in no mood to talk. When we finally caught up with him back at his flat later on, my presence didn't seem to help. He flew at me with a volley of abuse, ending with, "Look at him! He's *working* class![48] And can't even find his way out of a one-bedroom flat, for God's sake!"

While attempting to make a sharp exit, I had inadvertently opened the door to his closet, rather than the *front* door - something he used as ammunition and proof of my incompetence for several months after. Employing his sharp wits on this occasion, he made a quick getaway himself, somehow evading the 'professionals'; leaving us at the top of the stairs, or running down them, like slapstick Keystone Cops. Thankfully, before any damage could be done, he was picked up by the local, slightly more competent Police and transported to his allocated bed in the Parklands Mental Health Unit at the Royal Oldham Hospital.

My relationship with Mr L was strained for some time, and he bitterly rejected the rationale for being placed on a hospital ward, despite clear justification. He was highly elated at times and often confrontational. Barely tolerating my presence during the weekly ward rounds with the consultant, his mood remained erratic until the revised medication kicked in. In my experience, relationships with service users which start off badly and can be very challenging, are often the most fruitful ones in the long run. This was certainly the case with Mr L - the chemistry between us improving after his discharge from the hospital.

The introduction of Pia, a support worker, was a major catalyst in repairing relations. Mr L took to Pia well, and she had the ability to laugh off his more cantankerous behaviour - taking his dubious advice in a similar vein. An attractive woman of Italian origin, he informed her that her looks were wasted in this job; the alternative being "high-class prostitution" where she could earn far more. When she returned home to visit family, he recommended that she get an invite to the then President Silvio Berlusconi's infamous "Bunga Bunga" sex parties.

Mr L, out of sheer altruism, also counselled me...with career advice. He told me that I should try modelling. After a moment, basking in the warmth of a rare compliment, he then informed me, seemingly *without* irony or malice, "They have specialist agencies in Manchester for 'ugly models'. What with your bad teeth and everything, you could get jobs through them...Dickensian dramas maybe."

The state of my teeth was a favourite line of his. I once accompanied him to a dental appointment where, after a protracted period of treatment involving multiple fillings, he also had some teeth taken out. Leaving the treatment room, he announced to me and everyone in the waiting room, "Look at my teeth - they're nearly as bad as yours now!" Cheers Mr L.

~ ~ ~

Worked closely with Pia, we helped Mr L achieve more stability, thus stopping the never-ending, revolving door of hospital admissions. With help and advice from Kate too, a mental health nurse who had worked with him previously, we started to pinpoint the triggers which caused his relapses - trying to minimise these. Much of the work was small scale - practical help with household appliances for instance, such as making sure he knew how to use the TV remote control or the knobs on his cooker – but other tasks included organising his health appointments' schedule, plus helping to manage his finances. If these were out of kilter, he became incredibly anxious. Without the necessary concentration levels to immediately rectify such situations, Mr L often fell into a vortex of chaos, erratic mood swings and inescapable relapses.

A consistent feature or contributing factor to Mr L's 'relapse signature' was the use of alcohol. It was never particularly excessive, usually just a few drinks in the pub, but regular sessions led to relapse in the form of conflicts and scuffles. Alcohol countered the benefits of his medication, but having to warn him about the dangers of drinking was difficult for me given my liking of a pint; hypocrisy then being the only way forward.

Despite the sometimes-manic, surface bluster, Mr L was a caring and spiritual man. He regularly attended his local, Moravian church - one of the oldest, Protestant denominations in the world. Coming from an extremely prosperous 'old money' family, his ancestors had helped set up the church in Oldham. In his small, tower block flat - covered in pictures and his own artwork - were old photos, some faded, of various family members. When in a despondent mood, he would point out the contrast between his surroundings and the wealth of his extended family.

A highly talented artist, Mr L had a degree to his name, plus many prestigious art exhibitions under his belt. When he experienced the manic phase of his illness, his artistic output was prodigious - so much so that he even expressed his enjoyment of it. (Many have extolled similar virtues regarding the by-product of mania, including Spike Milligan, Vincent Van Gogh and Robin Williams.) Mr L's generosity was shown in the distribution and philanthropy of his artwork. He sent prints of his work to clinics, churches, constituency and councillor offices.

CMHT staff who had worked with Mr L could usually be identified by the artworks that populated their desks. There *was* a caveat to these gifts though. He would randomly give them away, but when in an indignant mood would frequently demand them back.

One of Mr L's favourite prints featured greetings in the five ethnic languages of Oldham - his way of bringing people together. Sexuality, invariably at the forefront when it came to his artwork, shone through in the form of 'Safe Sex' messages - shards of glass and condoms scattered among newspaper headlines about HIV/AIDS.

Some of the work that he gave away had a decidedly left field quality to it and addressed his sexuality in a very direct manner. He called this his "tasteful porn" collection. I still have, in my possession, a print showing a man in tight jeans sat on a phallic bollard; a 'Canal Street' sign underneath, with its C and S conspicuously absent. Given to me one Christmas, it was inscribed, "To Richard and all your family". A kind gesture, but I'm not sure what eleven-year-old Jasmine would have made of it.

Mr L's incorrigible and flamboyant nature was evident in the many stories he relayed to me about his past. These were often imparted whether I, or those nearby, liked it or not. In the 70s, after passing his Fine Art degree at Kingston University, he stayed in London and gained employment utilising his artistic talents. He worked as a set designer for various projects, including the famous children's television programme, 'Play Away'. He told many salacious tales regarding his time down south, and then later on in Amsterdam - most of which are unprintable. Among these were some of his supposed sexual conquests involving famous people who, despite his wishes, I will not name. I did not set out to write a kiss-and-tell gossip column, however entertaining these stories were, and don't particularly want to end up in court.

A favourite Mr L anecdote, which I dearly hope is true, is the time he sent Prime Minister David Cameron (c/o The Houses of Parliament) a package containing his soiled underwear. He insisted that this was a valid response given that he couldn't afford a new washing machine to clean said items; blaming Cameron and his government for this predicament.

In more elated moods, Mr L would tell tales at great speed, without pausing for breath, jumping from one subject to another (a common feature of bi-polar and known as a 'flight of ideas' or speech that is 'tangential' in its train of thought). The contrast between regaling us with such memories and his present reality - beset by loneliness - was great. Like many I've worked with, not least because of the erratic nature of their mental illness, Mr L and others had difficulty forming and maintaining relationships; often estranged from family members.[49]

For many years, while physically able, Mr L engaged in voluntary work at Cornerstone in Manchester - a charity which supports homeless people. He was a caring soul, always seeking to give something back, and I admire that about him. It was good for him also in terms of structure - enabling him to form relationships with people *outside* of mental health services. He told me about one of the friends he'd made - a fellow worker at Cornerstone whose punk, spiky, bleached hair and Dr Martens boots he loved. I think he always liked people who were a bit different - 'outsider' comrades.

On Christmas Day, he typically worked there, sharing a special meal with the homeless and his fellow staff. The alternative was staying at home…alone. I have rung him several times the day after he's come back from his volunteering activities and it always struck me how resilient and upbeat he was. It was especially heartrending since he was born and raised among a Christian congregation and family. Despite the importance attached to Christmas through his faith, Mr L still managed to maintain a cheerful demeanour, even while solitary. This image tugs at my heartstrings - then and now.

Mr L did have friends, and one in particular, Rachel, was extremely close. She lived in the same block of flats and was similarly afflicted with serious, long-term mental health problems. They were great support for each other and met, or spoke on the phone, daily. In fact, they were so enamoured, that they held their own marriage ceremony to declare their love for one aother. Despite her problems, when well, Rachel was most engaging, with a sharp intelligence and lively, warm, sociable manner. When *unwell*, she withdrew from life completely. The extreme, depressive episodes which she suffered overwhelmed her, leading to her taking her own life in April 2018. Accompanying Mr L to the funeral service was one of the saddest days of my working life. Although dignified in grief, the weeks after left him inconsolable. And he still expresses, with tears in his eyes, how much he misses her.

Later, that same year, Mr L also suffered the loss of his sister, Jill. Of all his family members, it was perhaps Jill that he was closest to. Older than Mr L, she had been frail for some time. This meant they hadn't seen each other for a while, but still managed to speak regularly over the phone. After a long battle with cancer, Jill finally succumbed to the disease. Although it may not have been a surprise, the loss of such a loved sister left Mr L crushed.

The cumulative effect of these losses, and their cruel timing, would be devastating for anyone, and so I had grave fears that this might lead to a major relapse in Mr L's mental health. Despite the grieving though and obvious vacuum in his life - where once there were loved ones - he seemed to cope remarkably well. His strength and fortitude in the face of such loss were admirable, but episodes like this rarely pass without long-term scars. I believe these experiences accelerated Mr L's aging process significantly.

There was a marked deterioration in Mr L's physical health. His scoliosis of the spine began to develop rapidly, leaving him with a bent posture that required the aid of a walker to move around. I had my aforementioned work wife, Danna, alongside me supporting him, and we now accompanied Mr L to many hospital appointments (frustratingly, the medical professionals said there was little that could be done to halt the growing damage to his spine). Aids to alleviate the effects of his condition, such as the walker, quite disgracefully had to be bought privately and were not, as I'd assumed, available free through the NHS.

One day Mr L collapsed in his flat and was admitted to hospital. The timing could not have been worse, for reasons that will become clear. He *had*, after a long wait, been allocated his own flat within an Extra Care Housing Scheme - ideal for his needs, as his eighth-floor flat was no longer suitable due to the deterioration of his spine. The move, alas, had to be postponed, even though the application had taken months. After his stay in hospital, he was transferred to Orchard Green - a short-term rehabilitation centre.

This latest episode took place during the first Coronavirus lockdown. Routine visits were therefore cancelled and communication with Mr L had to take place over the phone. In amongst this, heated conversations between myself and Orchard Green's management took place after Mr L was assessed by a 'genius' as fit for discharge *back* to his 8th floor tower block flat; a decision naively taken without consulting us - his care coordinators. The move was fortunately suspended following my protestations, making it clear it would be unsafe and counterproductive. The pressure to move him on from the facility was understandable, in the context of increased demand for beds due to the influx of hospital patients, but he already had the Extra Care room earmarked - appropriate to his needs – and so deviating from this path was insane.

Moving house at the best of times involves many tasks and much planning, and a seemingly infinite number of things can potentially go wrong. Supporting others relocating is difficult and includes a huge degree of responsibility, especially during lockdown when practically every task is met by an obstacle. In normal times we could commission staff from care agencies to help with the practical tasks such as packing. Conditions during the pandemic, however, meant the agency could not supply staff for anything other than emergency care (due to shortages). It was, therefore, left to Danna and me - kitted up in protective masks and clothing – to get stuck in. And it took nearly two full days, given the hundreds of pictures Mr L owned. On the second day, we arrived to find his door tragically open. Gingerly entering his flat, we found his treasured possessions scattered around - picture frames smashed and drawers left open with their contents on the floor. Mr L's flat had been burgled…while he was in rehab for fuck's sake.

After utilising our full bank of expletives, we contacted the local Police and the flat warden who arrived promptly to resecure the door. We then informed the staff at Orchard Green and broke the news to Mr L. He was, understandably, extremely upset.

No one from the Police contacted us in the immediate period after, despite us leaving our numbers. Obviously, in the circumstances, we didn't want to touch anything and interfere with the crime scene; we've all seen CSI! I decided to call the Police again and was informed that the case had been closed (*without* an investigation, as far as I could tell). This was despite the availability of CCTV footage at the flats and the wardens' knowledge of likely culprits (possibly residents). Whether this was one of the reported *80,000* crimes not properly investigated by Greater Manchester Police in 2020 - resulting in them being put into special measures - is a moot point. Either way, Mr L's discharge to his new flat was delayed once more.

Danna and I eventually cleared up the mess, arranged it into some kind of order – all without any outside help. Hiring a furniture removal company was difficult, as services like this were mostly frozen during lockdown. Danna did eventually find one though, who happened to be a relative of an ex-CMHT staff member. To plan the day, I asked our manager for additional staff to help with lifting and carrying, but she was unwilling to rubberstamp this due to staff shortages; a familiar echo by now.

The move went incredibly well. It was a herculean effort from the removal men, Danna and I, given the vast number of pictures and possessions. We finished before the planned time of Mr L's arrival. After calling Orchard Green, however, I was told that the ambulance needed to transport him to his new flat had only just been booked during a change of shift. Mr L would now arrive later on, rather than the morning as planned. You had *one job* to do!

Finally entering his new home, three hours later than scheduled, Mr L was welcomed by Rob, the manager of the scheme, and a well and truly knackered me. I had not been able to see him since his hospital admission due to Covid restrictions, so it was clear he had noticeably lost weight. Despite this, he was in good spirits though and seemed visibly cheered by his new flat – especially the carpet he had chosen. Many of his possessions were still packed away in boxes and bin bags, but this didn't dampen his arrival.

~ ~ ~

Lockdown over the winter of 2020 was a hard period for us all, although I'm happy to say that Mr L is well suited to his new flat. One of the attractions of the Extra Care scheme is that it allows him the autonomy of his own flat, with the added features of an in-house care team, plus meals from a central kitchen, and activities in communal areas where he can mix and meet others. Because of COVID-19 none of these 'extras' were immediately available when he moved in. I therefore commissioned an outside agency to support him, and this worked well. They have helped to turn his flat into a real home. And many of his pictures now take pride of place on his walls. I regularly phone Mr L and still visit him in his flat. He is disabled by scoliosis and severely restricted when it comes to mobility - a source of bitter frustration. He has also had to manage without Danna, who was on maternity leave. What of myself? Well, this was to be our last time working together. He now has a *new* social worker, who I trust will serve him well. Mr L has coped with change with great fortitude and good humour. He has also managed the brutal nature of lockdown's isolation far better than most. For this alone, even though he has many other qualities, he is a truly inspiring character; one that this bloody (ex) social worker is glad to have met. Long may he thrive.

As for me, the pressures of this underappreciated and overworked occupation during lockdown, helped propel me towards the exit door.

Chapter 14 - The End

June 15th, 2020

I wake up. Six emails today. The mental health crisis helpline has been busy. He needs help. He's asking for help. I'm his mental health social worker, but I'm staring at the emails feeling helpless.

Normally I'd go and see him. Get his sisters involved. We'd talk things through. Calm him down. And it'd be fine. I can't though. Because of the virus we're under strict instructions *not* to have face-to-face visits.

I ring him, knowing full well that he won't answer. He never does. And he doesn't this time. Two more emails. He's having thoughts about harming people again.

I ring his sister. No answer. I leave a message.

Another email. This time from the helpline manager. She asks that I account for my actions. Intervening. Visiting. Arranging appointments with the psychiatrist i.e. all the things we do during normal times.

What the fuck do you expect me to do *now*?

June 16th

Three more emails from the helpline about him. He's lonely and isolated, so they tell me. Never! Get away! Can I contact him and increase his care package? He has a package of daily visits, but agency staff aren't visiting at present because of the virus.

I email the psychiatrist and my manager, attaching all the correspondence.

I then ring his sister. Again. And manage to speak to her. She's not too worried about him. And the overriding impression I get is that he's bored.

The dragon of a manager gets in touch. "If nothing is done, I will escalate." Escalate – that beautiful word used by pompous arseholes.

Done? Like what? Sod it. Go for it, missus! And the best of luck getting a reply.

Amongst various other messages, I am asked by a neighbour to get someone's shopping in.

June 17th

Three more emails overnight about him. And two more expressing concern about others on my caseload. It's Wednesday morning at 10am. Sat on my bed, staring at a computer screen, I honestly don't know what the fuck to do.

My cat Benni nuzzles me for attention. I give her a cuddle and she looks up with sad eyes. I lose focus, then realise I'm welling up.

I can't go on like this.

~ ~ ~

Working from home during lockdown, dealing with the many daily issues which arise, certainly didn't help, but this wasn't the *major* reason for my decision to quit. Having the same responsibilities, without the usual means to intervene, felt farcical. And a good proportion of my caseload was difficult-to-engage males - hard nuts to crack - but I enjoyed trying. On the whole, I definitely worked well with this client group. The thing about 'difficult' males though is that they don't, in my experience, do phones very well. Face-to-face contact is essential. And there wasn't a lot I could do about that.

Truth be told - and that's what I'm here to do - my spark went out years before this. I was on a treadmill, doing the job because it paid the mortgage and bills - not really knowing a feasible way out. And I suspect there are many more in this rut than would care to admit it. I was now an older, experienced member of staff involved in the guidance and mentoring of young workers, but was increasingly conscious of my own weariness rubbing off on them.

I did the job well enough, but I didn't feel like I was making a *real* difference anymore.

Burnt out. There you have it.

This was 'The End'. Writing about the reasons is still painful, as I do not want them to overshadow the many positives gained during my social care days; or indeed overshadow the many inspirational stories I have featured in this book.

~ ~ ~

Death gives you perspective in life. During a brief period towards the end of my career, I experienced the death of my parents, and then an old school friend.

My dad died in Freeman Hospital in Newcastle - pancreatic cancer providing the last, fatal blow. The care he received in hospital was exemplary, but it is a cancer well known for its capacity to extinguish life. Two years later, my mam lost her battle against vascular dementia. During the final months of her life, she was ably cared for in a home; the staff wonderful. I was overcome with the kindness and empathy they showed my mother. This took place the year *before* Covid struck. Witnessing the horror of TV reports with elderly people dying alone in such homes - not even permitted the comfort of visits from family during their final hours - made me thankful for the time I spent with my parents before the end.

Losing one's parents as a middle-aged man is all part of the natural cycle of life. And it inevitably beckons a period of reflection. I was never particularly close to my parents, if I'm honest, during my adult life. Our relationship had many difficulties and problems. The periods of protracted illness before their deaths, however, at least gave me the chance to re-establish *some* form of connection with them; something I'm eternally grateful for. Complicated grief meant not just dealing with the inevitable sense of loss, regret and guilt, but also bitterness which came to the fore of my tumultuous, emotional state.

Even this did not prepare me for the death of my friend, Matthew, though; a man the same age as me. Then again, *nothing* could have. He had been my closest friend in sixth form at Wyndham School, and then later on at college in Liverpool. We lost touch, but I managed to see him again just before the onset of the first Covid lockdown and his battle with the cancer which would ultimately take his life. We had the chance to reminisce about our mutual struggles with school life, but also our happier memories of one summer (1988) spent in a flat in Southport; daylight hours spent washing up at a hotel, night time smoking, drinking and debating while listening to John Peel. Simple pleasures! I attended his funeral which took place in my birth town of Whitehaven, during lockdown, with only a limited number of people allowed to pay their last respects.

All three deaths made me reflect on the life that I'd built for myself. It's not so bad, I reckon. Natalie's family is my family now. And I love them all dearly. I'm alright. Don't cry. I consider myself lucky.

But the job. Oh, my bloody job…

~ ~ ~

Reflecting on thirty-two years grafting away in social care, it is impossible to express my feelings without looking at the bigger picture - namely, the changes that have taken place in wider society over this period. Looking back, I started my career at the *dawn* of the implementation of community care policies (around 1989), bringing with it a sense of uncharted territory and at least the *idea* that there could be progressive change in the way that society took care of its most vulnerable. Indeed, in the late nineties and at the turn of the century, I worked through a period of increased expansion of public services under New Labour. The policies and application of them may have been flawed, but at least there was hope and a progressive future to work towards.

By contrast, after a decade of austerity, there is now a corrosive sense of having discarded - or even forgotten - such noble ideals. At best, services are now planned around the central objective of managing the demise of the 'welfare state'.

I took up the role of union rep once again for my final three years or so. The local branch of Unison has suffered from a lack of ground level representation and I was the only union rep in the *whole* of adult social care - an unenviable situation which has now left a few branch officers running around like 'blue-arsed flies'. Working for Unison did provide some much-needed fire in my belly, but the all-pervasive apathy in the workforce concerning such matters didn't give me cause for optimism.

When each part of the system is eroded, the decay only spreads further. Resource shortages, leading to years on housing waiting lists, next to no access to clinical psychologists, or hours spent on benefit forms to achieve basic subsistence, all culminate in real and lasting damage to people's lives. And a consequence of this is that the Police, GP surgeries, housing providers and many others in resource-tightened professions are now asked to deal with people with complex mental health issues who no longer receive the *specialist* support they need. A synonym sometimes used for social worker is care coordinator. The policies of the last decade have led to this title becoming a misnomer, however. I did not coordinate services, but rather battled to cope given that there was a complete lack of them.

I am far from the only social worker taking the exit route. Many staff, most of them older with shedloads of experience, left during this recent period. Oldham Council, like others around the country, made a reported £8m worth of cuts in services when faced with a £30m shortfall in central government funding over the last, Covid-ravaged year. Further cuts are inevitable over the coming years to plug the funding gap. This is a far cry from what some understandably think, namely that 'There'll always be a need for social workers'. They're right, but there is a big divide between increased awareness and discussion about mental health, and the reality of frontline services which are slowly withering and dying off.

Cuts have a knock-on effect, as the lack of mental health services in the community increases pressure on already hard-pressed mental health wards and crisis services funded by the NHS. Despite reports in the media of increased mental health funding in recent years, those at the coalface rarely see tangible evidence of any improvement. In fact, it's quite the opposite.

Paying lip service to ideas stemming from communities, with emphasis on neighbourhood resilience and encouragement from senior management (using an 'asset-based approach') isn't the same as giving a damn, and so the job felt increasingly remote from the people we were set up to serve. It was as if the word 'community' had been axed from our designated brief as Community Mental Health Team. And compounding things in our case was the fact that our workplace was located on a remote Oldham business park, and it neither had the security nor soundproof spaces necessary for meeting people in a sensitive way.

I realised just how out of touch we were after speaking to my wife, Natalie, who worked at Positive Steps, a voluntary sector organisation based in the *centre* of Oldham. She engaged with a plethora of community groups, charities and resources which I barely knew existed. And it was another reason for my increasing sense of isolation and frustration with my job at the time.

For those of us who are a bit older and have 'been around the block a few times', there is the added sense of déjà vu triggered by the experience of previous funding cuts. And such a cycle leaves unsustainable gaps in provision, with corresponding pressure on the staff that remain; agency and other expensive forms of short-term staff thus crazily hired to plug the gaps. Result = increased funding = long-term contracted staff hired again = next round of cuts. Repeat. Anyone working in the public realm is all too familiar with this daft cycle.

As time went on, I most worryingly of all witnessed a change in staff culture. And I distinctly remember thinking, When did I become the old codger on the team? I had drifted along with the sense I was still one of the younger members, before the realisation hit me squarely in the face. The team camaraderie that I missed had been replaced by formulas; unsmiling, cost-saving initiatives and bean-counting 'brilliance'. Socially stingy people with equally stingy care packages. The same people rewarded with promotion!

In organisations that are increasingly resource-determined, individual teams become protective regarding their pool of assets and referral criteria for services becomes ever tighter. This inhibits working together just at the time when cross-team collaboration is needed the most. In recent years there have been many drawn-out legal battles concerning *which* authority/team is required to fund a particular service, especially when those who use services move to different areas. I promised at the start of this book not to go into boring detail about the mind-numbing anomalies of Section 117 of the Mental Health Act, which is the terrain on which these battles are fought, and so will happily fulfil my promise. *No more on the matter!* It is important to note, however, the time, resources and expertise spent fighting between ourselves which could be applied to more constructive endeavours, especially in the light of unmet needs.

I felt increasingly like a dinosaur because of my belief that social workers, emanating from radical, social philosophy, should attempt to function as agents for social change. The dominant discourse and daily, gruelling workload reflected a managerialist agenda though, based on short-term, costed utilisation with a limited focus on piecemeal changes for the individual. Tasks, in harmony with this, centred on routinised recording, data input, and use of IT assessment tools which limited the scope of everyday work.[50] This *feeding the machine* had an element of 'Big Brother is watching you' to it, but because the hardware was so out of date and unfit for use, it may as well have been Big Brother watching us through cracked pound shop glasses.

Rather than this way of working arising from actual discussion and consensus, it felt like cold, mechanical methods had become normalised - invidiously taking over, with little in the way of critical reflection. The practice of supervision also contradicted more instinctive ethics and felt a world away from the esoteric academia taught on the social work[51] courses, which challenged dominant ideas in an attempt to ramp up progressive, anti-discriminatory political values.

I was thus more and more aware of my apparent role as disgruntled 'Seen it all before, Heard it all before' old giffer in the corner. And now I've written the book!

~ ~ ~

Goodwill and charity should *not* be needed to replace the safety net provided by the seemingly outdated idea of a 'welfare state'. I am not critical of the increased role of the voluntary sector. I simply believe that these vital services should be an inalienable right and we shouldn't have to be reliant on the charity of others. To me, it is an indictment of our society that we cannot provide life's basics - such as food and shelter - to all our citizens as required. And when I hear senior managers refer to people who need our services as 'customers', it makes me think that Maggie Thatcher's vision is quite ludicrously still in the ascendency – Victorian values and all.

Recent media commentary described how the last Coronavirus-dominated year served to highlight rising inequality and a pernicious distribution of wealth in our society. The inexorable jump in homelessness and use of food banks brought into sharp focus the state of our public services. And such conditions were not created by a virus, but very evidently present long before this due to political choices.

My increasing frustration with the *limits* of modern social work is, in part, a result of these present conditions and the political context from which they stem. There is hope in the form of raised awareness regarding the crisis that exists, but this has not translated into political will i.e. decent wages for those who play vital roles in the sector (given the suffering and sacrifices they make). On a perhaps larger note, momentum has been given to the idea of a 'whole care' system, instead of the present division between the NHS and fractured, devalued social care services. It should not just be nurses that get deserved attention regarding wages and conditions, but rather *everyone* that participates in the provision of care services.

We are all interconnected and none of us can be certain if or when we will need vital care services. If the present era does not provide that necessary impetus for progressive change, however, then we will all potentially suffer.

It has been such a tumultuous time for all of us – both socially and work-wise - and experts have predicted a form of identity crisis as we adjust to a post-Covid/Lockdown world. I can relate to this, as when asked what I do now, I stumble for a response. However, this is an incredibly minor anxiety compared to the families/friends adjusting to their lives after having lost loved ones to this virus (150,000 deaths at the time of writing[52]). If anyone reading this is in that position, I can only offer my inadequate, but genuine condolences. I do know of people who have fallen victim to the virus. One was a much-loved colleague and mental health nurse at Tameside Hospital. Grant Maganga - Rest In Peace. I can therefore identify with the awful experience of not being able to personally share the sense of loss with those similarly affected, and the cold dislocation of digesting such news via social media only.

Paradoxically, lockdown - now that I am no longer in work - has given me the space to fulfil my ambition of writing a book. In what could be interpreted as the benign gesture of a higher power, I was fortunately bestowed the funds necessary for a lengthy break. Twenty-five years ago, I took out an endowment mortgage on the house I bought in Levenshulme. After selling the house, but not being au fait with how endowments work (like high-risk saving schemes), I received a cheque out of the blue which more than matched the sum I would have been entitled to if offered redundancy. Having no financial acumen whatsoever and certainly not paying attention to the policy detail at the time (not something that Martin Lewis would advocate), I seem to be on the *right* side of a scandal[53] for once!

Leaving a long-term job during these unprecedented times can be an underwhelming affair. There were no large gatherings of colleagues, speeches, or piss-ups in the pub. These normal 'closure' experiences were denied to me during this period. My departure was heralded by a few bottles of plonk, a hastily-remembered (and written) card with the price sticker still on it, and an unspoken IT'S ON MY WAY. After thirty-two years.

To be fair, once conditions allowed, I had several, momentous get-togethers with current and ex-staff, so I can't complain. Right now, I'm enduring the dying embers of a cold December in 2021, but doing alright. Thanks for asking! I'm still in touch with many of the characters in this book, including Mr L and Mr S, both of whom have chapters devoted to them. And they're doing well - touch wood.

I do not know what lies ahead. This is anxiety-provoking, but also strangely liberating. I feel for my former colleagues, still trying to stay afloat, in what is a profession and sector clearly in a state of crisis. I can only hope that social care's annus horribilis – or more accurately its *several* years of decline - acts as a catalyst towards a new realisation that society should concentrate on the things that matter. We shall see.

I hope you have enjoyed reading my story.

References

[1] Homophobia was one of Anderton's many abhorrent traits. Infamously, he was reported as saying AIDS was a punishment of gay people who were "swirling in a human cesspit of their own making". Anderton, known as "God's copper", was much-loved and subsequently received many awards from the incumbent Tory government.

[2] Nowadays, legal safeguards would need to be instituted for this to take place under 'Deprivation of Liberty' legislation (or DoLS, as it became known 'in the trade'). At this time, however, it was largely at the behest of management in individual homes.

[3] The use of nicknames is often discouraged in care settings, as they can be seen as demeaning. An example of this is J – a lovely woman who I worked with in a residential mental health facility - who others referred to as 'Sky'. I assumed this was because of her hippie-like clothes and outlook on life. I later learned that this was her nickname at a previous residence though, where she didn't interact with others and spent all day watching TV.

[4] The use of medication to treat, or in reality *control*, those with unidentifiable mental health conditions has received much adverse attention in clinical reports and via the mainstream media since, and is often disparagingly referred to as a 'chemical cosh'.

[5] Names and places throughout this book are anonymised for obvious reasons, with the exception of Michael. I sought permission for this from his wife, Sheena, who I am happily still in touch with via Facebook. Thank you, Sheena.

[6] Not to be confused with the present government's use of the phrase during Covid lockdown which, roughly translated, meant: "We'll do what the fuck we want, and you plebs need to abide by it and suffer in silence because you never learnt Latin at school."

[7] After the 1987 'Care in the Community' report, known as 'The Griffiths Report', many patients in these large institutions moved to smaller-scale housing provided and supported by local authority staff. Most of the large hospitals were subsequently closed, but some - like Calderstones - survive to this day, albeit with much-reduced numbers.

[8] Normalisation, although developed in Scandinavia, was prominent in America in the early 1970s and associated with mass deinstitutionalization following protests by patients and staff about systemic abuse in the large, old hospitals. It became the guiding light for community integration initiatives, directing policies which housed people within the wider community, allowing them access to mainstream services in health and education. It was practised widely in the UK, although sometimes crudely applied in order to curtail behaviour deemed negative to local communities (whose acceptance and tolerance had limits).

[9] The 1990 NHS and Community Care Act saw a huge rise and proliferation of social care services provided by the voluntary sector; something maintained since as the public sector has largely withdrawn from provision (apart from remaining statutory pockets). The Act marked the start of an 'internal market' whereby the NHS and local authorities would become 'purchasers' of services which they had previously, directly provided. Subsequent government policy - the Tories' 'Compulsory Competitive Tendering' and New Labour's 'Best Value' initiatives - augmented the voluntary sector's share of the health and social care market.

[10] The Lifeline Project was placed into administration in 2017 amid reports of mismanagement and financial irregularities. By this time, the company was big business with an annual turnover of £62m and had rapidly expanded in the previous decade, mainly as a result of winning contracts for public sector, outsourced services. Allegations made by staff regarding poor

management practice echo my earlier experiences. Instead of providing new, innovative services as it was set up to do, the business based itself on a parasitic model - reliant on government funding, replacing and undercutting existing services, until it finally overreached itself.

[11] Turning Point, since I worked there in 2003/4, has become one of the largest, voluntary sector providers in the country. Later, as a social worker in Oldham, I worked with the organisation as a commissioner of its services in mental health, in Supported Housing and Rehabilitation. Locally, they are now the chief providers of Substance Misuse Services.

[12] The Assertive Outreach Team model, like that of Community Mental Health Teams, employs people from different professions e.g. mental health nurses, social workers, occupational therapists and the like who work together in the same team. Unlike the traditional CMHT model though, cases are handled by the team rather than allocated to an individual; meaning, in theory, that stress and workload are shared equally. That's the theory anyway!

[13] An enduring myth when it comes to the criminal justice system and mental health is that 'do-gooders' help those charged avoid jail sentences by playing the eponymous 'mental health card'. During this early stage of my social work career, and indeed since, the exact opposite has been the case. Most of the time we are engaged in helping the person gain increased insight, plus take responsibility for their own behaviour. When charges are dropped, or not proceeded with, it is usually due to the reluctance of the Police or Criminal Prosecution Service to continue, whereas we often insist that the alleged perpetrator was not mentally ill when committing the said act. Social workers as 'hard taskmasters' does not fit the convenient, media stereotype, but it is much nearer the truth.

[14] It's common with cases well known to CMHTs - who achieve

a certain notoriety - to become the stock and trade for 'newbies'. The euphemistic logic behind such decisions runs along the lines of other staff having "done their bit" and the case needing "a fresh pair of eyes".

[15] Although the situation has improved over the years, old tensions can still easily be reignited. This was evident recently during a Coronavirus outbreak in town, when much of the conversation among the white population was dominated by a racial narrative blaming the Asian community for high infection rates in certain areas. Former members of far-right groups, such as the British National Party, undoubtedly played a part in stoking these embers under the shield of online anonymity.

[16] This allows a patient to be detained on a hospital ward for treatment of their mental health condition for an initial period of six weeks and *up to* six months following a Tribunal review.

[17] Disabled Living Allowance. This benefit was paid every fortnight. It was replaced by the Personal Independence Payment (PIP) in 2013.

[18] The ward round is a review meeting where the patient, in theory, gets to voice their opinion about their treatment and future options with those in charge of their care. In practice, ward rounds are often populated with too many staff members, which can make the whole experience quite impersonal and intimidating. The atmosphere of these meetings is also determined by the outlook and general mood that day of the all-too-powerful consultant psychiatrist.

[19] At this time we had plenty of 'in-house' support workers as part of the CMHT. Most of these posts have subsequently been cut, however, in favour of outsourced personal assistants who are cheaper (less wages, rights, training & no pension contributions) and generally employed on zero-hour contracts.

[20] The Phoenix Centre closed in 2008. The idea of day centres

was deemed old-fashioned by those in power and apparently "warehoused" those it aimed to support. The alternative set out was that people should use mainstream services in adult education – the idea being that they'd become less marginalised as a result. I believe the *actual* outcome of cuts like this though (in supported housing and clinical psychology) is increased isolation, depression and despair. And the sharp rise in suicide rates, witnessed in this country over the last decade, is stark evidence of this.

[21] Legal restrictions concerning those detained via acute hospital wards tend to be included in Section 3 of the 1983 Mental Health Act which states that a person can be initially held for up to six months before the need for a Mental Health Tribunal review. The majority of those on the forensic pathway, usually via prison, are on a Section 37/41. Section 37 defines the decision to hospitalise rather than imprison. Section 41 is the restriction level imposed when there are concerns about public safety. Although this is a slight simplification, these legal provisions are imposed in the majority of cases.

[22] This 'Panopticon' system of control, originally designed in the 18th century by social theorist and philosopher Jeremy Bentham, has been adopted by many prisons and asylums built since.

[23] In the early 1900s, this was the largest asylum in Europe - accommodating over 3,000 patients. Large parts of it closed with the onset of community care in the late 20th century, but its facilities have grown over the last 20 years with the introduction/provision of Low and Medium Secure Units.

[24] This situation was largely necessitated by high caseload levels and the finite resources of the CMHTs, meaning visits could not be conducted as much as I would have liked. It was one of the more frustrating aspects of the work as it hampered our ability to form therapeutic relationships with those on secure wards.

[25] Occupational therapists within CMHTs - and on wards - played

a vital part in this process. Their role was to assess basic daily living skills, set activities and measure the development of those preparing to function in a more independent environment.

[26] The Tribunal panel is chaired by a 'legal member' (often a circuit judge or senior lawyer), two 'medical members' (who tend to be psychiatrists) and a 'non-legal member' (with specialist experience in mental health). Attendees include the patient if they so wish, plus their solicitor and/or advocate (again, optional). The format on the day, after the panel has read the relevant reports, is to ask the professionals questions - usually in the order of psychiatrist, nursing staff, then CMHT staff, followed by a thorough grilling of the patient's solicitor (if present). The patient and family members (if present) are allowed to offer their point of view on the proceedings. The panel then retires to make its decision on whether the patient's detainment in hospital is justified under the auspices of the 1983 Mental Health Act.

[27] A cursory glance at social media posts reveals many opinions which can only be described as 'delusional', so there is no doubt that this is a subjective notion and continuum which many people are active within. An objective extreme exists, however, when those opinions take over every aspect of someone's life (to the detriment of their functioning and development). I can only assume that there are many who co-exist perfectly well in their normal lives, alongside believing that they are under constant surveillance by Bill Gates and that a cabal of paedophiles is controlling the mainstream media and plotting to create a worldwide virus hoax.

[28] The Secure Hospital sector was funded through the NHS Clinical Commissioning Group, but local authorities have responsibility for funding 'aftercare' under Section 117 of the 1983 Mental Health Act. There was much complexity and dispute between local authorities and CCGs in the application of this legal requirement, which I do not describe for fear of sending

readers into a nightmare-ridden stupor.

[29] RD Laing, in his celebrated study of schizophrenia in 1969, conceived 'divided self' to be the sufferer experiencing a personality disintegration following a 'double bind' conflict between contradictory messages from family and society relative to their own experiences of emotional pain. This is a distinctive and far more complex form compared to the idea of the 'twin personality'.

[30] Psychiatrists in Oldham are organised into certain sectors so that they see people from a specified geographical area.

[31] During conversations with Mr S in the writing of this chapter, he reviewed this part and told me it wasn't true. I imagined we were then going to have a difficult conversation where he denied such violence. What he actually objected to was me mistakenly saying it was a brick, and so he corrected me, informing me that it was in fact a claw hammer. It's good to be accurate!

[32] There is much controversy around Clozaril, because of its potential side effects, which can be damaging and sometimes fatal. Patients require stringent monitoring and must attend a specialist clinic for blood tests once a week for the first six months, and once a month thereafter.

[33] This is often referred to as a 'Section in the Community' as it allows for a quick recall to hospital if the conditions of the order are not fulfilled. These often specify that the person engages with the treatment offered, takes medication as prescribed and refrains from the 'harmful use' of alcohol and/or illicit drugs.

[34] After this time, lack of access to clinical psychologists became a huge problem for CMHTs in Oldham. Waiting times became prohibitive and, to my mind, this reduced the quality of interventions we were able to offer.

[35] Cognitive Behavioural Therapy (CBT) aims to help people become aware of their negative interpretations of the world and

thus develop alternative ways of thinking about situations, plus take action which can reduce their distress. The Cognitive Analytic Therapy (CAT) approach analyses past events and relationships that underlie present problems in thinking and behaviour. Both approaches involve creating manageable goals or, as June called it, her 'homework'.

[36] I have always been pragmatic with bending rules in certain situations. I take inspiration for this from a sadly-departed friend, Steve. He was a well-known and highly regarded teacher. At his funeral, his colleagues all wore T-shirts with the letters 'DIMDIF'; his nickname, signifying his favourite phrase when reacting to irritating, bureaucratic diktats - "Does it matter? Does it fuck!" Steve Price. Much missed. RIP.

[37] I observed that when June did something, she always did it to the extreme. This leant towards the popular hypothesis of 'addictive personality'. It's a term rarely used by professionals within care services, as there is an absence of evidence to support such a notion. There is also the fear of this label becoming a self-fulfilling prophesy and the belief that they have no control over their impulses, thereby inhibiting any motivation to change.

[38] The function assigned under Deprivation of Liberty Safeguards (DoLS) to assess the advantages and disadvantages of an individual resident's freedom to leave the home without supervision being curtailed, and to decide whether any such measure was a 'proportionate response' to the risks that they may face in the outside community.

[39] Another top tip to residential home managers – never employ multiple members of the same family and especially those from your *own* family. It tends to breed cliques within the team and has been a chief characteristic in many safeguarding investigations that I have been party to. Oh, and another one - try not to piss off the visiting social worker.

[40] Mental Health is different from other forms of disability in that

it is usually not visible, and the degree of its disabling effects fluctuates. There is increased complexity in providing information on one-size-fits-all benefit forms for those with mental health issues therefore. For example, those who suffer psychotic episodes may have better days (when functioning at a good level) than those who cannot even dress themselves due to distractions and disturbances in their mind.

[41] The team at Oldham had many memorable characters. One that I remember with great sadness is Alison Howe, who was tragically killed in the 2017 Manchester bombing while waiting to pick up her children from the MEN Arena. She is remembered for her kind and empathetic manner, and was a credit to her profession. She was a true nurse in the best sense of the word. Alison Howe RIP.

[42] This team was part of the CMHT setup in Oldham and, as the name implies, my work involved reviewing care packages and commissioning service providers in both the private and voluntary sector.

[43] I worked alongside the very capable, in-house support worker, Phil (part of the CMHT, employed by the NHS), who carried out the majority of visits, while my role was mostly in a reviewing capacity. Given the choice, I preferred working with support workers from *within* the CMHT, as this was essential for close team work and communication - a great benefit when dealing with potentially high-risk individuals. Unfortunately, such 'comfort' became increasingly rare due to the severe reduction in public sector, employed support workers in mental health teams, both locally and nationally.

[44] These theorists emphasise the social causes of mental distress and consider the institution of psychiatry a tool of social control and a coercive instrument of oppression. In this scenario, social work is seen as the velvet glove (acting for the iron fist of psychiatry and Police) within a system of control and repression.

I accept that this is a somewhat crude simplification, but it represents Mr W's core concerns.

[45] Social workers don't have the right of access to people's financial dealings, and rightly so unless they are placed into 'Appointeeship' with the local authority. This only takes place when a person has had financial difficulties e.g. debt trouble or the incapacity to deal with financial affairs.

[46] Bi-polar describes a disorder of extremes, with fluctuations in mood that switch from a depressed state to an elated and often hyperactive one. Mr L exhibited pressured speech (speedily switching from one subject to another), emotional extremes and disinhibited behaviour (with little or no consideration of risk). These phases, however, were not always clearly differentiated, and I came to observe in Mr L extremely low mood combined *with* manic behaviour.

[47] An informal or voluntary admission is the preferred option, as this gives the person some control over the decisions being made about their life. In a scenario, however, where that person is so consumed by their condition that they do not notice their precarious mental state or resulting behaviour and thus cannot appreciate the concomitant risks (referred to as "lack of insight"), then a Mental Health Act Assessment or Section route must be taken.

[48] Mr L's laughable snobbery knew no bounds when he was ill. When well, he was reasonable, and chortled about such an attitude though. He can still be contradictory, but lovable with it.

[49] In cases where someone is socially isolated, it is difficult to stop them becoming dependent on the staff who support them. And in the long-term case of Mr L, it becomes impossible, however laudable the aim.

[50] I have hardly written about the bread-and-butter, core tasks that characterise this most beleaguered of professions. There's

been barely a mention of risk, capacity and needs assessments which are the bedrock from which support is accessed. No space has been devoted to the ever-changing, convoluted, safeguarding processes and case conferences facilitated to protect those that we serve. In my defence, I do not apologise, but reiterate that this book is ultimately about my experiences with *people* rather than *processes.*

[51] I've also not given any attention to the training and social work theory which is meant to guide our practice. Primarily, this results from my view that models such as the task-centred (TC) approach or crisis intervention are more after-the-fact, descriptive approaches and therefore offer little guidance concerning what to do in the midst of complex situations actually faced. I don't remember ever thinking 'I'll use a crisis intervention approach here', referring to a textbook for relevant advice.

[52] Data from March 2020 onwards:
https://coronavirus.data.gov.uk/details/deaths

[53] Endowment mortgages: Legacy of a Scandal
https://www.bbc.co.uk/news/business-20858236

Milton Keynes UK
Ingram Content Group UK Ltd.
UKHW021331260424
441819UK00018B/114

9 781739 668129